KEEPING HOLY THE LORD'S DAY

By Gabriel Meyer

"There is not now space to treat of these ages . . . which shall be brought to a close, not by an evening, but by the Lord's Day, as an eighth and eternal day, consecrated by the Resurrection of Christ and prefiguring the eternal repose not only of the spirit, but also of the body. There we shall rest and see, see and love, love and praise." St. Augustine, ***City of God***

A City of the Lord Publication

Phoenix • Los Angeles • San Diego • Monterey

© **Copyright** City of the Lord, 2016

All rights reserved. For permission to reproduce or copy, contact City of the Lord.

Publisher: City of the Lord

711 W University Drive

Tempe, Arizona 85281

480-968-5895

www.cityofthelord.org, PhoenixBranch@cityofthelord.org

City of the Lord is officially established as a Private Association of the Christian Faithful and Private Juridic Person of Diocesan Right by Bishop Thomas J. Olmsted, May 8, 2012. City of the Lord is also a founding member of the Catholic Fraternity, a private association of the Catholic faithful, established in the Vatican by Pope Saint John Paul II on November 30, 1990.

Printed in the United States of America.

Keeping Holy the Lord's Day

Written by Gabriel Meyer

Cover Artist: Jim Hyde

Image of the Holy Face—http://manoppello.eu/eng/index.php?go=historia

Unless otherwise stated, all scripture quotations excerpted from Revised Standard Version of the Bible—Second Catholic Edition (Ignatius Edition) Copyright ©2006 National Council of the Churches of Christ in the United States of America. Used by permission. All rights reserved.

ISBN—13-978-0-9915327-1-1

www.keepingholythelordsday.com

Table of Contents

Foreword 5

Introduction: Remember the Lord's Day . . . ? 6

Chapter One 12

    Why Keep Holy the Lord's Day? 12

    Life 14

Chapter Two 18

    The Lord's Day and the Eucharist 18

    The Resurrection 19

    The Eucharist 21

Chapter Three 27

    The Lord's Day and the Family 27

    Culture radiates out from the family 28

    Where do you start? 30

Chapter Four 32

    Honor 32

Chapter Five 39

    Rest 39

    Work and Rest 42

Chapter Six 46

    Leisure 46

Chapter Seven 52

    Joy 52

Chapter Eight: 59

    Peace 59

- Peace Equals Right Relations 61
- The Art of Contentment 63

Chapter Nine 65

- Mercy 65
- The Eighth Day 70

Chapter Eleven 77

- The Lord's Day in a Post-Christian World 77

Bibliography 82

- Inaugurating the Lord's Day 83
- Living the Gospel as a Way of Life 83

Foreword

For many years I have wanted this book to be written. And I knew Gabriel Meyer was the right person to write it. As a founding leader of the Los Angeles branch of our covenant community, Gabe led the effort to encourage making observance of the Lord's Day a building block of our life together. It was Gabe who brought the celebration of inaugurating the Lord's Day with a Saturday family meal to us, a story he relates in this book. He was the one who reminded us that Sunday should have a rhythm that differs from the rest of the week.

So I asked him, "Why keep holy the Lord's Day?" He answers that question marvelously in the pages of this book. You will enjoy reading it, and if you take its advice, I know you will enjoy keeping the Lord's Day. It will become your favorite day of the week, just as it is mine. If you are willing to "…set aside this day from every care and sorrow", Sunday will be a safe port in the storms of your life. It will become the day that reminds you that we are going to live forever in the presence of God, so the trials of this life will be kept in the right perspective.

If keeping the Lord's Day has been burdensome for you, or if you've really never even tried to keep it holy, you will be encouraged by this book. The author explains that honoring the Lord's Day is so much more than a rule to be kept. Do you need more peace in your life? How about joy and mercy? You will find these virtues in the keeping of the Lord's Day. There are many blessings for those who honor the Lord by honoring His day.

Several years ago, I bumped into a member of my community I hadn't seen for a while. I asked him where he'd been and what had been keeping him away from our Sunday community gathering. He told me that he was so busy with work that he needed Sunday afternoons to catch up. I challenged him to trust God with Sunday. If he would give God one day, God would help him to get all his work done on the other six days. He took the challenge and found very quickly how generous our Lord is. He became a great advocate for keeping holy the Lord's Day. I make that same challenge to you.

Sincerely,

Bob Carmody, Overall Coordinator of City of the Lord, 2005-2012

Introduction: Remember the Lord's Day . . . ?

It may seem a startling, if not extreme assertion with which to begin this little booklet on the Lord's Day, but I'm going to make it anyway: Keeping the Lord's Day is an essential starting point in the practical renewal and reinvigoration of Christian life, in the renewal of the Christian family and in the creation of genuine Christian community.

If anyone were to ask me: What can I do to start building a vibrant Christian life in my family? Keep holy the Lord's Day would be my reply.

If anyone were to ask: Where does parish renewal begin? We all know that many things go into that endeavor, but, among them, I would say: Keep holy the Lord's Day.

If a good Catholic were to complain to me that his or her life lacked joy, I would not hesitate to urge: Keep holy the Lord's Day.

Now that I've got your attention (hopefully), let's talk about the aims of this little booklet.

First of all, full disclosure: What I'll try to outline in the next pages reflects the experiences of City of the Lord, a Catholic charismatic covenant community, headquartered in Tempe, Arizona, with branches in Los Angeles, Monterey, and San Diego, California. Many years ago, Pope Saint John Paul II urged lay communities not to keep the gifts they had been given to themselves but to share them with fellow Catholics.

"Open yourselves with docility to the gifts of the Holy Spirit," the Pope urged. "Do not forget that every gift [you have received] is given for the common good, that is, for the benefit of the whole Church."

In the years following this remarkable meeting with the Pope, community leaders have tried to take his message to heart and to discern those elements in our life as a Catholic lay community that could be of most benefit to fellow Catholics at large, in parishes, convents, monasteries, and in other Catholic movements.

Some years ago, we published a short manual, "Living the Gospel as a Way of Life" by James Jones, one of the community's founders, which outlined the "building blocks" of Christian culture. This was our first attempt to "translate" aspects of our community experience into teaching that could speak to the needs of fellow Catholics in a wide variety of pastoral situations.

This book, "Keeping Holy the Lord's Day," is a companion volume to that effort and focuses on another signature aspect of our experience as a community: celebrating the Lord's Day.

The custom of inaugurating the Lord's Day goes back to the earliest days of City of the Lord and is one of the elements out of which our life developed – and not ours alone. Some form of the Lord's Day celebration – and there are many variations – is part of the life of many communities that emerged from the Catholic charismatic renewal and in recent years has been adopted by students and student groups on many Catholic campuses around the country. It is not too much to say that the Lord's Day is one of the aspects of the particular wisdom God has given us as a community. It is one of His gifts and which, with its focus on building out from the family, has deeply influenced the way we think about Christian culture.

As with the teaching on Christian brotherhood and sisterhood in the previous book, the vision of the Lord's Day explored in these pages stands at the very center of Catholic life.

The Lord's Day is the original feast day, and it should be proposed to the piety of the faithful and taught to them in such a way that it may become in fact a day of joy and of freedom from work. (Vatican II, Constitution on the Sacred Liturgy, V:106)

"*The Sunday celebration of the Lord's Day and His Eucharist is at the heart of the Church's life.*" Catechism of the Catholic Church, CCC 2177

This revival or restoration of the genuine observance of Sunday as the Lord's Day stands as one of the principal items on Vatican II's ongoing agenda for the spiritual and cultural renewal of Catholic life. And here the Church is aiming for more than attendance at Sunday Mass and the feasts of the liturgical year – that's just the start. What's involved is something much larger and more encompassing: that is, adopting a fully developed liturgical and sacramental frame of mind. This means more than attending a few seminars or boning up a bit on liturgical theology.

The Church, in the vision of Vatican II, is calling for the renewal of the intrinsic culture of Catholics: to open up the way we live and spend our time to the redemptive work of Jesus; to see our lives here and now in the light of the Passion and Resurrection and to allow the Holy Spirit to refashion our whole mentality, patterns of life, use of time, cultural norms, even the character of our emotional and affective life in accordance with Christian truth and in the light of the "eternal perspective."

No single element is more central to this effort, to this Catholic cultural recovery, than the restoration of the culture of Sunday as the Lord's Day – a vision of weekly renewal, refreshment, rest and peace.

For me, forty-two years ago, the vision of the Lord's Day as one of the keys to Christian life came both as a surprise and something of a revelation.

In 1973, a number of us involved with the Catholic charismatic prayer group at Loyola Marymount University in Los Angeles traveled to South Bend, Indiana and Ann Arbor, Michigan in order to see for ourselves what was happening in the foundational lay communities in our still-youthful movement.

It proved to be a pivotal experience for us and led, a year later, to the formation of the lay community which became City of the Lord, now headquartered in Phoenix.

But of all the many impressions and lessons we took back with us from our tour of intentional communities, the one that had the most revolutionary (and immediate) impact on us was the experience of celebrating the Lord's Day.

In The Word of God community in Ann Arbor, Michigan, leaders there had developed a comprehensive approach to honoring Sunday as the Lord's Day. It began on Saturday evening, in community homes, with a brief table ceremony, which involved lighting candles in honor of the day and passing around a loaf of bread and a glass of wine along with appetizers at the beginning of the meal, which was also graced with special prayers.

Brothers and sisters, this is the Lord's Day. Let us welcome it in joy and peace. Today we set aside the concerns of the week in order to honor the Lord and celebrate his Resurrection. Today we cease from our work in order to worship God and remember the eternal life to which he has called us. . . .

Everyone in the household or family was required to be present for these Saturday evening meals, and, in fact, people told us that they wouldn't think of missing them, that these celebratory evenings were the highlight of the week. As one person told me, unforgettably, that night so many years ago, "The Lord's Day is like a harbor – I can get through the roughest week knowing that this awaits me, that the Lord's Day is there."

In the course of the leisurely meal, the husband acknowledged and thanked his wife, the parents blessed each of their children, and those at the table shared about the events of the past week and encouraged one another. Not that the table talk was "heavy" or "pious" in any way. On the contrary, conversation was light and positive, and regularly "enlivened" by bursts of spontaneous singing – simple refrains that everyone knew and, in some cases, special songs sung only on the Lord's Day.

After the meal, family members spent the evening together, often inviting neighbors or nearby parishioners to join them in a relaxed round of games or, during special seasons like Advent or Lent, a discussion of a book the household had decided to read and reflect on together, or simply to continue the informal dinner sharing in small groups. Since it was summer in Michigan when we visited the community, people took advantage of the balmy nights to take walks in the neighborhood, calling in on neighbors as they passed.

The next day, after attending Mass together, the family snacked on a buffet of leftovers and enjoyed a relaxed afternoon. Some people read quietly; others went on hikes with friends; others visited sick and home-bound members of the parish, bringing meals or just a little company on a Sunday afternoon.

As sunset approached and the challenges of the upcoming week began to make themselves felt once more, the household gathered together to bid farewell to the Lord's Day with a brief closing prayer:

Sovereign of the Universe, Father of mercy and forgiveness, grant that we may begin the working days which draw near to us in peace, freed from all sin and transgression and living in the joy of Your Holy Spirit. . . .

A candle which had been lit the evening before at the start of the Lord's Day was ceremonially extinguished. Everyone wished each other "a good week!" before turning, refreshed, to the looming responsibilities of the workaday world.

While the particular ways in which charismatic communities did (and do) honor the Lord's Day are not sacrosanct, what is worth noticing, and what certainly impressed us so many years ago, is the idea – the essential idea that to keep holy the Lord's Day is to set it apart, to spend it differently than one spends the other days of the week, to live a different way on that day – relaxing the schedule, spending quality time with the people you love, refreshing oneself in the perspective of eternity, in what is finally important.

Secondly, the idea of the domestic church, that one's home can (and must) be a place of spirituality and prayer and worship – this had a revolutionary impact on all of us. Here we had found a group of people who were translating the ideals of Christian life into a spiritual culture lived out in the home and in the context of ordinary family life. Far from a dour, dutiful business in which family members had to be force-marched into faith, what we saw those many years ago was relaxed, at ease, and joyful.

That's what impressed us most, I think, the joy – the idea that Sunday, for Christians, was to be a day of joy, singing, and celebration, a weekly experience of the reality of the Resurrection. In the Lord's Day we're challenged to put aside the troubles of the week, the stresses of work, the worries about children, money, and the future that preoccupy most of us 24/7 and taste, if only for a day, the joy and freedom of Christ's victory.

"So, then, there remains a Sabbath rest for the people of God; for whoever enters God's rest also ceases from his labors as God did from his. Let us therefore strive to enter that rest." Hebrews 4:9-11

The purpose of this booklet is to help Catholics appropriate the riches of the Lord's Day in their own lives, parishes, convents, and families. The perspective I draw on, of course, is my own and reflects the experience of charismatic covenant communities around the world. The point, however, is not to promote any particular set of approaches and customs, but to offer our experience as an encouragement for other Catholics to develop their own ways to keep holy the Lord's Day, and in the context of their particular situations and circumstances.

In addition, these pages will attempt to provide a rationale for setting aside the Lord's Day as a special weekly "sanctuary" (the "why") and enrich these observations with the testimony of Scripture, the Church Fathers, the teaching of the magisterium and the Catechism, along with some helpful insights from Jewish "Sabbath" traditions.

The Lord's Day, in the end, is not only a practical instrument in the building of strong Christian family, and in the enrichment of parish life; it presents us with a vision of what the Christian life looks like, what genuine Christian leisure is, and how to be empowered in real time with the joy of the Risen Lord.

PART ONE: FOUNDATIONS

Chapter One

Why Keep Holy the Lord's Day?

One of the first, if not *the* first question a contemporary person poses to an invitation to do anything outside the realm of personal inclination is – *why?*

That even applies here, perhaps especially here when we are considering a practice the Church warmly encourages but which is, increasingly, out of step with the pace of today's world and its priorities.

Why keep holy the Lord's Day? Why go to the trouble of special meals and special prayers outside of Sunday Mass attendance? It's fine for those who are interested in that sort of thing, who have the time. But what's the point? What is this supposed to do for me and my family?

Since keeping the Lord's Day, as I'm proposing it here, involves a lot of changes and a lot of challenges, "why" is not such a bad place to start. Modern families will need to be persuaded of the potential benefits of the Lord's Day if they are to take the considerable trouble to expand its observance beyond attendance at Sunday Mass, and incorporate its values and blessings into their lives.

In a very real sense, this whole booklet is an attempt to respond to that "why," to lay out a broad rationale for building or restoring a Sunday culture in today's Catholic family, parish, and community.

Having said that, my inner curmudgeon insists on pointing out that honoring the Lord's Day, for a practicing Catholic, is a serious matter. It is, in Christian terms, the fulfillment of one of the Ten Commandments:

"Remember the Sabbath day, to keep it holy." Exodus 20:8

I also can't resist adding that the Old Testament takes a very hard line on the subject:

"[Moses said to them:] Six days shall work be done, but on the seventh day you shall have a holy Sabbath of solemn rest to the Lord; whoever does any work on it shall be <u>put to death</u>." Exodus 35:2

It is also one of the Precepts of the Church:

"On Sundays and other holy days of obligation, the faithful are obliged to assist at Mass. They are also to abstain from such work or business that would inhibit the worship to be given to God, the joy proper to the Lord's Day, or the due relaxation of mind and body." Code of Canon Law, 1247

A sterner attitude would seek a rock-bottom motivation for "keeping holy the Lord's Day" less in demonstrable benefits than in obedience to the Lord and conformity with the norms of Catholic life.

But now that I've got that off my chest, it's worth saying that even here, it's vital to see the commandments of God and the precepts of the Church not simply as expressions of duty and obligation, but – more importantly, as conduits, vessels of <u>the full life</u> that God wishes to give His people.

This latter point is worth underlining, – especially at the outset of our discussion of the importance of the Lord's Day. Undergirding all that God requires of us in the Christian life – even the things that are difficult – is the invitation to life – abundant life, not only in the world to come, but in the here and now, in the midst of the ordinary realities of our lives.

At the heart of that invitation to life is the invitation to give our lives to Him, to the life-giver, to commit ourselves personally to the Lord. Like all aspects of Catholic life, the Lord's Day finds its context in the call to holiness, in the personal submission of our lives to God. Keeping the Lord's Day is not magic – it is one of the instruments of God's grace to make us, step by step, as the First Letter of Peter, echoing Exodus, proclaims:

"…a holy nation, God's own people, that you may declare the wonderful deeds of him who called you out of darkness into his marvelous light." 1 Peter 2:9

It's vital that we see exploring the culture of the Lord's Day in the light of following the Lord more deeply and building what Pope Saint John Paul II has strikingly called a "civilization of love."

Another essential preliminary: All that we attempt in our Christian lives begins and ends with the grace of the Holy Spirit. Enriching our observance of the Lord's Day is no exception. The various models or approaches we'll consider in these next pages are merely the scaffolding, the frameworks into which the Spirit pours His life and grace. The results – life, joy, rest, peace – are the signs of his handiwork and, it should be stressed, the fruit of earnest prayer.

Life

One of the obstacles that we have to confront right at the outset has to do with the impression that keeping holy the Lord's Day is fundamentally about restrictions – about *not* doing things. Older Catholics can still remember "blue laws" that persisted in various parts of the country, that restricted shopping and sales of alcohol and that shuttered most restaurants and public venues on Sundays.

For many people, a generation or two ago, Sunday was mostly about what you couldn't (or shouldn't) do.

The Lord's Day is not about restrictions and a lot of arbitrary rules; it is, in fact, about life – the good, abundant, and meaningful life that God wishes to impart to us -- not only in eternity, but now, in this world, in our families, convents, and parishes.

The point about "this world" deserves a small digression: One of the most powerful insights in G. K. Chesterton's meditation on the philosophy of St. Thomas Aquinas involves his critique of the mistaken notion that "spiritual" means "immaterial." (An early charismatic renewal preacher once critiqued this common attitude by quipping that "Fred was so heavenly that he was no earthly good.") In fact, as Chesterton, via Genesis, noted: God, having created the world, looked on all things and saw that they were good.

"*There are no bad things, but only the bad uses of things. . . The devil cannot make things bad; they remain as on the first day of creation. <u>The work</u>*

<u>*of heaven alone is material – the making of a material world*</u>. *The work of hell is entirely spiritual."*

The point here is that God (or heaven, if you will) employs the material things of our world; He speaks through them, and works through them. That the "good life" to which the Lord's Day draws us – a good life that joyously employs the things of earth – should be the means through which we are drawn to love the things of heaven, should not surprise a Christian in the least.

Too often we're content to make do, spiritually, to settle for so much less than God wishes to give us.

Years ago, a priest friend of mine, confronted with a chronically unhappy parishioner, chided him that his problem was that he was starving in the midst of abundance, content to crawl around under the table of grace, living off the crumbs.

"Don't you know that there's a banquet just a few feet away and there's a place there for you at the table with your name on it? Why are you crawling around on the periphery of God's grace? Take your rightful place at the feast -- and eat."

This is the theme that runs through the many Gospel accounts of Jesus's healing on the Sabbath. Rather than focusing on the restrictions of the Sabbath, Jesus emphasizes, and demonstrates, its potential for life, healing, and restoration.

To cite just one example: In the speech Jesus delivers following the healing of the man born blind on the Sabbath (John 9), He instructs the astonished crowd that He has come into the world to care for and pastor His people:

"I came that they might have life, and have it abundantly." John 10:10

It is no accident that these episodes of healing occur in the context of the Sabbath "rest" (see Luke 4:31-39; Mark 6:6-11; Luke 13:10-17; John 5:1-18, etc.) and that they result not merely in spiritual solace for sufferers, but in concrete liberation and physical well-being in the here and now.

The sharp rebukes that the Sabbath legalism of some Jewish leaders draw from Christ also serve to emphasize that the day of rest is meant to be not a mesh of pious restrictions but one of openness to the life and power of God.

As the Lord, in the prophecy of Isaiah, promises:

"If you turn back your foot from the Sabbath, from doing your business on my holy day, and call the Sabbath a delight and the holy day of the Lord honorable; if you honor it, not going your own ways, or pursuing your own business, or talking idly; then shall you <u>take delight in the Lord</u>, and I will make you <u>ride upon the heights of the earth; I will feed you with the heritage of Jacob your father</u>, for the mouth of the Lord has spoken." Isaiah 58:13-14

This passage from Isaiah hearkens back to the Song of Moses in Deuteronomy in which the Law-giver reminds the people that fidelity to God brings abundant life in its wake:

"The Lord made him ride on the heights of the earth, and he ate the produce of the fields; and he made him suck honey out of the rock and oil out of the flinty rock; curds from the herd and milk from the flocks, . . . with the finest of the wheat – and of the blood of grapes you drank wine." Deuteronomy 32:13-14

Again, this imagery reminds us that when we give our lives to God, when we choose to live as He directs, He gives His own life to us in response – in Jesus's words:

"…good measure, pressed down, shaken together, running over will be put into your lap." Luke 6:38

The biblical notion of the Sabbath promises something far greater than the practical benefits of a day-off once a week. It is a weekly recovery of the meaning and purpose of life, a day lived not only in the perspective of eternity, but in its joy and abundance.

As the great Jewish philosopher Abraham Heschel writes in his classic study "The Sabbath":

"The Sabbath as a day of rest . . . is not for the purpose of recovering one's lost strength and becoming fit for the forthcoming labor. <u>The Sabbath is a day for the sake of life</u>. Man is not a beast of burden, and the Sabbath is not for

the purpose of enhancing the efficiency of his work . . . It is not an interlude but the <u>climax of living</u>."

Chapter Two

The Lord's Day and the Eucharist

"The Sunday celebration of the Lord's Day and his Eucharist is at the heart of the Church's life." CCC:2177

Beyond all considerations of the benefits of Lord's Day observance, we need to remind ourselves of first principles: The purpose of the Lord's Day is to allow for the celebration of the central act of Christian worship – the weekly Sunday Eucharist.

A story from the early Acts of the Christian Martyrs provides a powerful witness to this truth. A priest brought before a Roman magistrate is rebuked for summoning an "illegal" assembly of believers on Sunday:

When the protoconsul said to him [the priest Saturninus]: "Against the decree of the emperors and caesars you have called an assembly of these people," the presbyter Saturninus, inspired by the Spirit of the Lord, respondsed, "Surely we have celebrated the supper of the Lord." The proconsul: "Why?" Saturninus: **"Because it is impossible** *for us not to celebrate the supper of the Lord."*

So central is this connection – between the Lord's Day and the Eucharist – that every element of the day, all liturgical expressions, all domestic prayers and customs, find their orientation, power, and meaning in the Eucharist.

This is one of the reasons, and only one, why the Lord's Day is not the same as the Jewish Sabbath or a wholesale transference of "Sabbath" spirituality to another day of the week. The Lord's Day is a uniquely Christian observance.

There are two reasons for this: the Resurrection of Jesus and the Eucharist.

The Resurrection

The Jewish week started with what we now call Sunday (the first day of the week) and ended with the Sabbath – the day of rest which recalled the second chapter of Genesis in which God "rested" from the work of creation (Genesis 2:1-3). Jewish Christians, in the first decades of the Church, continued to observe the Sabbath as a day of rest and attended the synagogue for the traditional Sabbath prayers and the weekly Torah reading. But by the end of the first century, Sunday, as the special day to celebrate the Lord's Supper had become something more than the "first day of the week" for Christians. It had its own distinctive character as the "Lord's Day."

We find this already in the New Testament.

At the end of the Gospel of Luke, we find the account of the revelation on the way to Emmaus, where the risen Jesus joins two dispirited disciples as they walk home (Luke 24:13-35). This event occurs on the afternoon of the Sunday of the Resurrection ("that very day," 24:13). Unrecognized, Jesus reminds these disciples of what He had taught them about the meaning of His suffering and death and leads them through a catechesis of Old Testament scriptural passages:

"And beginning with Moses and all the prophets, he interpreted to them in all the scriptures the things concerning himself" (Luke 24:27). A later reference to Jesus's messianic catechesis also includes the *Psalms* (Luke 24:44).

This "liturgy of the Word" culminates in "the breaking of the bread," in the course of which the disciples recognize their Master (Luke 24:30-31). It doesn't take much imagination to recognize in the outlines of the incident an evocation of the Eucharistic liturgy itself, in which the explication of the Word leads to the revelation of the Lord's presence in the "breaking of the bread."

That all this takes place on Sunday, the Lord's Day is significant, not only in terms of the historical details of the story, but in terms of the recognition by the earliest Christians of the linkage between Jesus's Resurrection and a unique Christian assembly on that day.

We find the Lord's Day mentioned explicitly in the Book of Revelation. This is in the context of John's vision of the end of history and the final triumph of Christ and His people, which takes place "on the Lord's Day" (Revelation 1:10). This is not a mere incidental detail, but points in the direction of a fuller meaning of the day, as an anticipation of the glory that will be revealed at the end of time:

"Hallelujah! For the Lord our God the almighty reigns. Let us rejoice and exult and give him the glory, for the marriage of the Lamb has come, and his bride has made herself ready; it was granted to her to be clothed with fine linen, bright and pure." Revelation *19:6-8*

All these connections are rooted in the reality that Christ's Resurrection occurred on the first day of the week, on Sunday. The Resurrection of Christ from the dead is not merely an isolated marvel, but, as the early Christians saw, the start of a new creation, the renewal of the whole of creation in the triumph of Christ over what St. Paul rightly calls, "the last enemy," death (1 Corinthians 15:26).

In this sense, as Vatican II urges, each Sunday is to be seen as a little Easter – a taste of the freedom Christ has won for us over the limitations of human nature and, human frailty, over the limitations of time itself.

"And I heard a loud voice from the throne saying: 'Behold, the dwelling of God is with men. He will dwell with them, and they shall be his people, and God himself will be with them; he will wipe away every tear from their eyes, and death shall be no more, neither shall there be mourning nor crying nor pain any more, for the former things [literally, the "old order"] has passed away.'" Revelation 21:3-4

Hence, the early Church was not long content to permit the Sabbath day, Saturday, with its reminiscences of the first creation to remain the pinnacle of the week, but to insist that the new creation, inaugurated in the risen Christ, and to be revealed in its fullness at His Second Coming, should form, for the Christian, its apex and crown.

As one well-known liturgist puts it: "Easter is to the course of the year exactly what Sunday is to the course of the week: It is the great festival of salvation."

The Eucharist

In fact, early on, the principal element determining how Christians spent the Lord's Day had less to do with notions of "Sabbath rest" and the cessation of labor than with the need to set aside Sunday morning for this "festival of salvation," for the Eucharistic assembly.

That those Sunday liturgies were not the "efficient" hour-long Masses of today is made abundantly clear in the early literature. At the end of the fourth century, the intrepid Spanish nun Egeria, on pilgrimage, gives a rich picture of the Sunday Liturgy in Jerusalem. It began at daybreak and ended shortly before noon! In Jerusalem, the Sunday Eucharist was considerably lengthened by the local custom of allowing each priest present to preach, if he chose – this, no doubt, because of the presence of so many international pilgrims. Each group was permitted to hear the Word of God expounded in his or her own native tongue. After a leisurely noon meal, there was Vespers at four!

But even without the special situation of Jerusalem, parochial liturgies in the West usually involved neighborhood processions to the church with banners and crosses for worship services that would take up the better part of Sunday morning and be followed by festive meals, coupled with Eucharistically inspired generosity to the poor.

As fourth-century Church Father John Chrysostom would urge:

"You cannot pray at home as at church, where there is a great multitude, where exclamations are cried out to God as from one great heart, and where there is something more: the union of minds, the accord of souls, the bond of charity, the prayers of the priests."

Since the dawn of the liturgical movement in the Catholic Church nearly a century ago, the restoration of Sunday and the spirituality of Sunday, the Lord's Day has been a major piece in the reform of the Church's liturgy. Many of the Vatican II liturgical reforms had, as a principal object, the clarification of the liturgical preeminence of Sunday worship and its connection to Easter. These reforms also aimed at the enrichment of Sunday Mass with a more generous selection of Scripture readings and, through the addition of new Eucharistic prayers, a richer Liturgy of the Eucharist. Vatican II also looked forward to the recapturing of what we might call the "culture" of the Lord's Day – if not the day-long liturgical exertions of the patristic age, at least to a fuller appropriation of the spiritual potential that the Lord's Day holds for Catholic life.

"Hence, the Lord's Day is the original feast day, and it should be proposed to the piety of the faithful and taught to them in such a way that it may <u>become in fact a day of joy and of freedom from work</u>." (Vatican II, Liturgy V: 106)

If, as we've affirmed, the Eucharist is the heart of the Lord's Day, then the purpose of other customs and observances we employ on this day have to do with either preparing us for the Sunday Liturgy or providing us with opportunities to reflect on, enhance, or live out the implications of our Eucharistic worship.

The Lord's Day culture I attempt to describe in this booklet is entirely about making the Eucharist more in our lives, releasing its power, and letting the "engine" of Eucharistic worship permeate the way we spend our Sundays, even when we're no longer at church.

If we inaugurate the Lord's Day on Saturday evening, for example, in a family setting, preparing for the Sunday Liturgy is at the heart of why we do this. It should be noted here that those who customarily participate in the Saturday Vigil Mass can also incorporate aspects of the domestic inauguration of the Lord's Day into their Saturday schedules, either before going to Mass or upon returning.

In this spirit, many families who celebrate the Lord's Day focus the day's activities around reflecting on elements in the Sunday Mass:

- Preparing for Mass by reading aloud the Scripture readings at dinner the night before, or during Sunday morning breakfast

- Reflecting together on the various Eucharistic prayers before going to Mass as a way of deepening the appreciation of the Liturgy

- Sharing together reflections on the Sunday Gospel or on insights gleaned from the homily.

Inaugurating the Lord's Day on Saturday evening, however one does it, brings alive the notion of <u>liturgical time</u>, which commences traditionally at sunset, and establishes in our households, as an element of practical life, one of the deepest aspects of Catholic culture: the experience of the sanctification of time.

Rather than employing time simply on the basis of work-related imperatives ("what I have to get done") or, worse yet, on the basis of whim and fancy ("this is what I feel like doing now"), by "sanctifying," or setting aside time for the Lord, we create what Jewish philosopher Joshua Abraham Heschel calls "an architecture in time." We carve out a temporal space in which, no matter what we may feel at that moment or what life may have brought us during the week, we invite God to be with us and to anchor us once more in his redemptive life and truth and joy.

It would be hard to exaggerate the practical importance of recovering this liturgical sensibility in our lives.

Those of us who regularly set apart the Lord's Day can easily recall times in which it was not easy to switch from the mood our work and relationships had brought us to by the end of the week and embrace the joy of Sunday. Perhaps there had been chaos at work, or the children had been hard to handle or a relative had been hospitalized, or we had "blown up" once again at the "difficult" neighbor next door. It's tempting to say, when faced with preparations for the Lord's Day meal, "I just don't feel up to this tonight."

But to do that, I've discovered, is to miss the redemptive role that a liturgical life can play in our lives – and even in our emotions, in the way we feel.

The liturgy, in all its aspects, is about bringing the redemptive life of Jesus to bear on the circumstances of ordinary life. By setting aside, or "consecrating" times and seasons, we remove ourselves from the ever-changing, shifting demands of the workaday world and enter into the saving dimension of Reality with a capital "R." This is what the Apostle Paul means when he prays for the Ephesian community that

"...the eyes of your hearts [may be] enlightened, that you may know what is the hope to which he has called you, what are the riches of his glorious

inheritance in the saints, and what is the immeasurable greatness of his power in us who believe." Ephesians 1:18-19

How many times have I entered the Lord's Day with a heavy heart only to find that, in its environment of joy and peace, I was eventually able to put aside the cares of the week, and anchor myself, not in the emotions of the moment or in the problems or failures of the day, but in the reality and power of Christ's "indestructible life." Hebrews 7:16

In the Byzantine Liturgy, there is a powerful hymn that bridges the shift from the Liturgy of the Word to that of the Eucharist. Modeled after the vision of Isaiah 6, it urges worshipers to see themselves in the midst of the service as "representatives" of the cherubim, the creatures who surround the throne of God. In order to "see" the invisible presence of Christ, and enter the reality into which the Liturgy invites, worshipers pledge to "lay aside all earthly cares."

"Let us who mystically represent the Cherubim, and who sing the thrice-holy hymn to the life-creating Trinity, now lay aside all earthly cares, so that we may welcome the King of all, who comes invisibly upborne by the angelic hosts. Alleluia."

Even on the psychological level, it's supremely healthy to experience, at least once a week, that we and our problems are not the center of the universe. God is. And to experience, if only for a few hours, what it might mean to lay down our preoccupations and taste the freedom Christ has won for us, as an associate says, "to live on this day the way we will live on That Day!"

In fact, in one of the community households I lived in many years ago, the leader of the household always exhorted those at table to leave their troubles at the door. He would light-heartedly advise that everyone leave his "bag of cares" in the hallway. "You can pick them up again after the Lord's Day, if you wish."

Finally, the culture of the Lord's Day is Eucharistic in a moral sense as well: Lord's Day culture is a culture of thanksgiving.

In referring to culture, I mean that "thanksgiving" is a great deal more than managing a few words of appreciation now and then. It is a basic attitude toward life, a spiritual outlook – so basic in fact that, over time, it grows into what might well be called the "eucharistic personality," the person who is thankful.

This, of course, is the goal, on the personal plane, of receiving Communion – we become that which we consume. As St. Augustine wrote to catechumens, playing on the various meanings of the phrase "body of Christ",

"*Let you therefore receive and eat the Body of Christ: you who have now become the members of Christ in the Body of Christ. . . <u>Begin to receive that which you have begun to be.</u>*"

The fundamental characteristic of the eucharistic personality, as exemplified by Jesus Himself, is gratitude for all that God has placed in our lives and, with that, an ability to give thanks even in difficult circumstances, even in the midst of suffering (see Psalm 116).

Gratitude and thankfulness, in this sense, is not wishful thinking or "whistling in the dark." It is based, in fact, on a realistic assessment of who we are, and the character of the real situation we are in. Ingratitude, by contrast, is a form of spiritual blindness, fed by illusions and the resentment born out of our inability to manufacture the lives to which we imagine we're entitled. As a friend of mine often says, "No one really sees his life for what it really is until he or she is prepared to be grateful for it, as it is."

Once we realize the truth of who God is, and who we are, and begin to grasp the depth of His love for us, our whole lives become an act of gratitude to God for all that He has done, all He is doing, and all that He will do for us. When we become part of God's people, we become a people whose very life, meaning, and purpose is gratitude, thanksgiving, and praise.

The Lord's Day can play a helpful role in the process of becoming thankful people. In addition to the more direct connections with honoring the Eucharist which we've noted, this moral dimension of gratitude, one of the principal effects of Eucharistic worship, is at the heart of the Lord's Day practices.

The Lord's Day allows for less hurried blessings surrounding meals. Even the notion of saying a blessing not only before but <u>after</u> meals can be a novel experience for some nowadays. The experience of a leisurely family meal is itself an opportunity to grow in gratitude for family life and relationships. The service closing the Lord's Day gives thanks for the gift of Sunday rest and peace.

A culture of thanksgiving permeates each of the Lord's Day practices. Naturally, this is not meant to be a one-day-a-week experience, with the other six days happily given over to complaint and ingratitude, but a prototype, an image of how we might live our whole lives, if we choose.

The early Christian theologian Origen alluded to this "training" aspect of the Lord's Day in his assertion that the goal of Sunday observance is the life of contemplation, the perpetual feast day:

"The perfect man who is always with the words, the actions, the thoughts of the Word of God, is always living in His days, and all His days are Lord's Days."

Chapter Three

The Lord's Day and the Family

"Sunday, the Lord's Day, is characterized by a fruitful and effective remembrance of God's saving acts. The Word of God cannot be absent in family life. Coming together around the Word of life thus becomes a privileged occasion where the family, the domestic church, finds itself fully in the Liturgy of the Christian community." Jubilee of Families, 2000

We referred above to Pope Saint John Paul's notion of a "civilization of love," and, from time to time, in this study of the Lord's Day, we allude to "spiritual culture" or to the cultural building blocks of Catholic life.

But what do we mean by a "spiritual culture"?

In our society, when we use the word "culture," we often mean "cultural pursuits," as in leisure-time activities. But the word as we're using it here encompasses a great deal more than that.

<u>Culture is a design for living</u>, a way of life that encompasses the whole breadth of the human enterprise – morality, personal relations, family, courtship, celebration and mourning, sanctity of time, conflict resolution, piety, manners. Culture, then, is not a limited set of activities, but the whole of life.

What this booklet suggests is that Catholics have a culture in this sense, too. Not an ethnic culture, but a universal spiritual culture, one pertaining to every Catholic, that includes the moral dimension, but goes on to embrace the practical implications, in real-life circumstances, of being a baptized person and living the life to which the sacraments point, and which they empower.

This is an important point because it helps us overcome the limited notion that being Catholic is just a matter of entertaining certain beliefs, or seeing to it that my kids go to Catholic schools, or just showing up to church most Sundays. Christianity is a whole way of life, a distinctive way of being in the world.

The Catholic writer Caryll Houselander puts it well:

"Our life is sacramental. We do not live that peculiar thing one hears so much of, a 'spiritual life.' We live a natural and supernatural life; we live it through the medium of the simplest substance of things. Our Lord gave Himself to us through our flesh and blood; we give ourselves back to Him through it. The symbols of the gift of His own life are bread, wine, water and oil. We give our life back to Him through the dust He made us out of, through everything we see and touch and taste and hear, the food we eat, the clothes we wear, the words we speak, the sleep we sleep. Such are the sacramentals of our love, things ordinary with the ordinariness of the risen Christ."

Such a universal culture, formed by the sacraments, is a spiritual culture, that is, one inspired, shaped, graced and sustained by the Holy Spirit, whose work it is to form in us the character of Christ and teach us the culture of the kingdom.

Culture radiates out from the family

<u>Family is the heart of this spiritual culture</u>. Family is also the heart of the Church and the school of life and the virtues to which the Holy Spirit leads us. To summarize: building Christian culture radiates out from the family.

As the Catechism states:

"'The Christian family constitutes a specific revelation and realization of ecclesial communion, and for this reason and it can and should be called a domestic church.' It is a community of faith, hope, and charity; it assumes singular importance in the Church, as is evident in the New Testament. . . It is called to partake of the prayer and sacrifice of Christ. Daily prayer and the reading of the Word of God strengthen it in charity. The Christian family has an evangelizing and missionary task." CCC:2204-2205

There is, in fact, no substitute for the family as the "engine" of the Church, the seedbed or nursery of its life and witness.

It should come as no surprise to us, then, that one of the reasons Christianity is in something of a societal crisis today has to do with the cultural eclipse of the family and of family-centered life. Throughout history, the family has functioned as the privileged place for the transmission of the faith. If the family falls apart or becomes, in cultural terms, a shadow of itself, the Church will suffer internal weaknesses as well as the external challenges such weaknesses invite.

Family scholar David Popenoe describes the situation in the starkest terms:

"The abrupt and rapid change in the situation of families and children that began in the 1960s caught most family scholars by surprise. . . This period has witnessed an unprecedented decline of the family as a social institution. Families have lost functions, social power, and authority over their members. They have grown smaller in size, less stable and shorter in life span. People have become less willing to invest time, money, and energy in family life, turning instead to investments in themselves."

Popenoe's portrait of the "disappearing family," dire when he made it at the end of the last century, has, if anything, worsened beyond recognition in the decades since.

This family eclipse, so evident in the cultural trends of our day, manages, for the most part, to fly under the radar of much current analysis and strategic thinking about the situation of the Church, which tends to emphasize program and activity-based solutions rather than organic ones built on re-envisioning and re-equipping the Christian family.

If the family is indeed the heart of Christian culture – and it is – then one of the essential first steps we must take in rebuilding Catholic life in our day is to restore families and family life – <u>to reinvest in the family</u>. A major part of this process involves restoring the traditional functions of the family – particularly the family as the center of life, culture, piety, training and education, the center, in other words, of the cultural transmission of Christian life.

It's a daunting task that won't be accomplished overnight, even by a single generation, let alone a single community or movement. But if efforts aren't made to restore and refresh family life, then our other efforts at renewal, however well-intentioned, will, ultimately, fall short.

Where do you start?

In my experience, you start by <u>restoring the family as a center of prayer</u>. Restoring the family as a center of religious culture and tradition – as a place not only of teaching and training but also of prayer and celebration – this is the first and most vital task. It is a matter of grounding the family, often in very basic ways, once more in God.

As the Catechism reminds us:

"The Christian family is the first place of education in prayer. Based on the sacrament of marriage, the family is the domestic church where God's children learn to pray 'as the Church' and to persevere in prayer. For young children, in particular, daily family prayer is the first witness to the Church's living memory as awakened patiently by the Holy Spirit." CCC: 2685

Many older Catholics remember festive family celebrations on the major feasts and on the saint's days of children, weekly family rosaries, prayer before and after meals, and the regular use of sacramentals such as holy water in the home.

Now, this is not a plea for nostalgia or a return to what we imagine was a better and simpler past. But it is a recognition that establishing family traditions of prayer, piety, and celebration constitute an essential element in passing on the faith from generation to generation, and in the restoration of the full reality of the Christian family itself.

The fact that many Catholics, even regular church-goers, no longer have the experience of a vital domestic religious culture, or, indeed, of a domestic religious culture of any kind -- who, in effect, live in largely secularized home environments seven days a week -- may account for the lack of vitality in whole sectors of American Catholic life.

Clearly, considerable ingenuity and imagination will be required to establish a culture of prayer in the contemporary Catholic family; but it must be done – and it must be done knowing that the heart of this enterprise is, as the Catechism powerfully observes, praying <u>"as the Church"</u> and witnessing "to <u>the Church's living memory</u> as awakened patiently by the Holy Spirit." Fortunately, the Lord has not left us entirely to our own devices in this effort.

The Lord's Day is one of the most effective tools I know for building Christian culture in the family, any family, and for developing an approach to family prayer that is oriented not simply to the immediate needs of its members, as important as those are, but to positioning the life of the family in the heart of the Church's own life. Thus, the family becomes a witness to her living and redemptive memory, to the liturgical and sacramental mentality to which we referred earlier.

Less a set of prayers than a whole orientation, the Lord's Day helps establish spiritual and relational patterns in the family that have the potential, in time, "awakened patiently by the Holy Spirit" and with the reasonable good will of its members to help reshape, enliven, and enlarge family life itself.

The next section of this booklet will explore seven aspects or "facets" of the promise of the Lord's Day. In the course of these chapters, we will detail various ways in which family life (along with parish, convent, and community life) can be shaped and enriched by a fuller observance of Sunday's liturgical and sacramental possibilities.

It is well to be reminded, especially at this point in the discussion, that building family culture and establishing good Christian traditions in our homes is not really about our efforts, however conscientious, but about God's. We are not the ones who establish the way of life or construct the culture; it is God who creates a life for His people.

Developing traditions that impart life across the generations is a spiritual operation and not a matter of cultural engineering; it's a matter of receiving a life from the Lord, of allowing the Holy Spirit to bring to concrete expression all that God has for us in the life of the Church.

But there is more.

We are witnesses to the life that comes with surrender to God and to His will. But, as the Lord's Day highlights, the life that God is teaching and forming in us is only a shadow of the fullness of that Life that will be revealed in the kingdom of heaven.

PART TWO: FACETS

Chapter Four

Honor

Christian culture is a culture of honor.

Let love be genuine; hate what is evil, hold fast to what is good; love one another with brotherly affection; outdo one another with showing honor." Romans 12:9-10

While the word "honor" has a slightly dated feel about it, considering our individualistic and egalitarian society, it is a very important reality in Scripture and in classical Christian thought.

Honor, basically, refers to two things:

To the value or worth of someone or something; and

To the outward expression or manifestation of that worth or esteem.

So, in terms of the quote cited above from Romans, Paul is urging that Christians both acknowledge each other's "worth" in the eyes of God and express that acknowledgement openly as part of what it means to love as an essential aspect of the love and affection that should characterize their relationships.

Both attitude and act are essential here. Honor is not only something you think (attitude); it is something you do (act). The two – attitude and act – must go together. For example, it is clearly inadequate and wrong to believe something to be of supreme value in your heart (attitude) but to treat it with neglect or abuse in your actions. And, conversely, to honor someone (act) without really believing in his or her worth (attitude) is called flattery.

Beyond this strict definition of the word, I have always found the way the distinguished charismatic leader Charles Simpson describes honor to be particularly helpful: "Honor is the atmosphere or attitude of community." Honor is the attitude and the behavior that, together, make relationships work. As the Apostle exhorts, honor is an aspect of love.

One of the most important passages on honor in the Bible is one of the most familiar: The Ten Commandments in Exodus 20 (1-17). These commandments, which outline fundamental biblical principles about the way of life God wishes to teach His people, revolve around the theme of honor.

We honor God by refraining from treating anyone or anything else as if he or it were God, or using his Name in a fraudulent or frivolous way (commandments 1-2). We honor parents, who gave us life and sustenance (commandment 4). Honor is also the key to the other social commandments (5-10): We honor life (which, since you did not give it, is not yours to take); we honor the reputation, possessions, spouses (life commitments) of others (which, in that they belong to someone else, are not yours to appropriate, misrepresent, or alienate).

At the pivotal point in those commandments (commandment 3), when they move from the honor due to God to the honor due to parents and others (the social commands) is the commandment to "remember the Sabbath day, to keep it holy."

"Six days you shall labor and do all your work; but the seventh day is a Sabbath to the Lord your God; in it you shall not do any work, you, or your son or your daughter, your manservant or your maidservant, or your cattle, or the sojourner who is within your gates; for in six days the Lord made heaven and earth, the sea and all that is in them, and rested the seventh day; therefore the Lord blessed the Sabbath day and hallowed it." Exodus 20:8-11

There is a great deal to explore in this passage, but suffice it to say for our purposes, the principal motivation behind the commandment has to do with honoring God. The reason the day is "hallowed" or set apart from other days is centered on honoring the "rest" of God. This has less to do with a literal view of the Genesis six-day creation story than with the notion of thanksgiving for God's work in creation, in "remembering," and therefore celebrating (and honoring) the mighty deeds of God. In that sense, the third commandment (in the Catholic numbering) is linked to the first two commandments that have to do with honoring God's unique being and role in the world and honoring His name. In the Sabbath commandment, we honor His life-giving deeds as creator and savior.

This redemptive aspect is true even in later Judaism, where, in addition to celebrating creation, the command to "remember" following Deuteronomy 5:15, is thought by medieval Jewish commentators to apply to God's saving deeds in the exodus from Egypt, the divine act that resulted in the creation of the people of Israel.

When early Christianity took over some of these themes in the evolution of Sunday as the Lord's Day, not surprisingly, it shifted the focus away from honoring the first creation to honoring an even greater set of mighty deeds -- the "new creation" inaugurated in Christ's death and Resurrection.

For Christians, the first creation, wounded by the sin of Adam and Eve, is haunted by death and decay. It is the "old order" that is even now passing away in the light of the kingdom to come (Rev. 21:4).

As Athanasius the Great wrote in the fourth century:

"But when a new people was created, it was no longer necessary for this new people to observe the end of the first creation, but rather to seek the beginning of the second. And what is this but the day on which the Lord rose again. It is from here that the new creation began, of which St. Paul says, 'If, then, anyone is in Christ, he is a new creation.'"

But, however great the shift from the focus of Jewish Sabbath to the Lord's Day, what we do on Sunday must still be seen, as in Exodus 20, in the context of honor: Honoring God for what He has done for us in Christ, for the life we have as His people, and for the final victory of the kingdom to come.

And, as we saw above, in the definition of honor, this involves something more than a few fleeting thoughts of gratitude; that inner thanksgiving must find expression in behavior, in the form of culture.

Another aspect of honor particularly associated with the Lord's Day has to do with honoring the people in our lives, particularly in our families. This is evident in the Ten Commandments in which honoring God's "rest" on the Sabbath also involves ensuring that the blessings of Shabbat are shared by each and every person in the family. Even slaves and hired hands are invited to share in the sanctity of the day, a revolutionary gesture in Roman times, an affirmation of fundamental human equality before God, sojourners and foreigners, too. (Exodus 20:10). Livestock and beasts of burden were permitted to rest, prefiguring the harmony between humans and the rest of creation that would mark the messianic age.

"The wolf shall dwell with the lamb, and the leopard shall lie down with the kid, and the calf and the lion and the fatling together, and a little child shall lead them. . . The suckling child shall play over the hole of the asp [serpent] and the weaned child shall put his hand on the adder's den. They shall not hurt or destroy in all my holy mountain; for the earth shall be full of the knowledge of the Lord as the waters cover the sea." Isaiah 11:6-9

In many charismatic communities, the various domestic Lord's Day customs provide an opportunity to honor relationships in the family. Fathers and husbands, wives and mothers, children – all are acknowledged and blessed in the course of the domestic prayers of the day. As we noted above, it isn't enough simply to entertain an inner respect for your one's parents or children, toward those whose commitment and labor sustain us, who carry on our life and heritage into the future. Honor isn't really honor until it is expressed, until it is explicit, until it has become behavior.

Expressing honor in the family is also an important part of the education and formation of children, in learning how to express appreciation for the gift of their parents, and to honor the specific contributions each member of the family makes to its life.

Cultural patterns in our society do not make open, unambiguous expressions of affection and esteem very easy. We've all been brought up in a culture that finds open expressions of respect embarrassing – to be deflected by a nearly instinctive resort to self-deprecating humor.

We can all remember, too well perhaps, episodes in our childhood in which attempts by adults outside the family to praise our accomplishments or appearance were countered by thoughtless, though good-natured familial put-downs.

Still more serious are those late discoveries in life by parents that their children did, in fact, recognize and honor the sacrifices they made to raise them – recognition disguised, however, under a generation of family wisecracks and ribbing.

One of the tasks of building a Catholic culture is to break through the barriers those patterns create and to learn to relate to one another in an environment of open affection and praise, a praise not simply based on performance, but also on the roles that people play in our lives.

In many community settings, the inauguration of the Lord's Day on Saturday evenings provides a natural opportunity to acknowledge the contributions of all members of the family, affirming in a clear and unmistakable way the covenantal character of the Christian family and the unconditional bonds that hold it all together in the mercy, kindness, and love of God.

Again, this is recognition given regardless of whether parents feel that they've been "star athletes" as parents that week, or whether children have behaved like angels. The honor due to parents is not conditioned on perceptions of their success, nor is the honor and respect due to children conditioned on their performance as family assets.

In this context, the weekly or even daily blessing of children by parents is vital. Honoring family members on their birthdays or other occasions of special importance is part of basic spiritual health and also as an example of the family's role as an emblem of unconditional love.

The Lord's Day ceremonies developed by covenant communities over the past nearly half-century have all tended to highlight the role and contribution of women in the family, particularly the work and ministry of mothers. Given the gender-oriented tensions in our society and the ambivalence our secular culture shows toward the role of women in the family, underscoring the vital importance of the contribution of women is both a corrective to cultural attitudes and a formative witness to the truth. This, of course, is not to dismiss in any way the essential contributions husbands and fathers make to the family.

Borrowing from Jewish tradition, many versions of the Lord's Day inauguration around the dinner table include the recitation of Proverbs 31, the scriptural hymn to the virtuous wife. While some contemporary women have been known to dismiss Proverbs 31 as a suspiciously enthusiastic "celebration" of housework, a closer and more objective examination of the passage reveals it not only as a hymn of praise for the indispensable work women do in the home, but also as a recognition of women as strong, capable, provident and gifted partners in the family-building enterprise.

> *A good wife, who can find?*
> *She is more precious than jewels.*
> *The heart of her husband trusts in her,*
> *And he will have no lack of gain.*
> *She does him good and not harm*
> *All the days of her life . . .*
> *Strength and dignity are her clothing,*
> *And she laughs at the time to come.*
> *She opens her mouth with wisdom,*
> *And the teachings of kindness are on her tongue.*
> *She looks well to the ways of her household,*
> *And does not eat the bread of idleness.*
> *Her children rise up and call her blessed;*
> *Her husband also, and he praises her:*
> *"Many women have done excellently,*
> *But you surpass them all."*
> *Charm is deceitful and beauty is vain,*
> *But a woman who fears the Lord is to be praised.*
> *Give her the fruit of her hands,*
> *And let her works praise her in the [city] gates.* Proverbs 31:10-31

In addition to the proverbial portrait of the wise and industrious wife, we cannot fail to notice the "culture of honor" manifested in the passage. Here, children praise their mother; the husband praises his wife, and not only in the bosom of the family, but at the city gates where public life was conducted in the ancient world.

A practical note: Festive Lord's Day meals can be a lot of work – work that is too often invisible to those who enjoy them. It's not helpful if the virtuous wife is praised at the table but too exhausted by all the preparations to enjoy the festivities along with her family. It takes a little organization, but everyone should help out with the preparations and serving so that no one ends up effectively excluded from the "rest" appropriate to the day. Jewish tradition is helpful here: On Shabbat, a special stew is traditionally prepared ahead of time, a hearty dish that can remain on the stove and be served throughout the day, thus keeping kitchen prep time down to a minimum.

The Lord's Day has proven over the years to be a particularly effective way for many families to introduce elements of honor and an atmosphere of praise and esteem into the fabric of modern Catholic family life -- and this without a lot of awkwardness and fuss. The idea, of course, is that what happens on Saturday evenings or Sunday afternoons gradually (and with wisdom and patience) becomes a life-giving part of everyday life and a heritage of love to be passed on to future generations – that honor and praise, as we noted at the beginning of the chapter, becomes the relational "atmosphere" that we breathe.

Chapter Five

Rest

"Come to me, all who labor and are heavy laden, and I will give you rest. Take my yoke upon you and learn from me; for I am gentle and lowly in heart, and you will find rest for your souls. For my yoke is easy and my burden light." Matthew 11:28-29

This famous and comforting saying of Jesus, with its echoes of the Beatitudes ("blessed are the poor in spirit", etc.), comes just before chapter 12 of Matthew's Gospel and its focus on controversies about the Sabbath.

As we have already seen, the keynote of Jesus's attitude about the Sabbath is that its observance should not be focused on restrictions (what you may not do) but, on the contrary, on what God is doing and will do for His people -- on the life, healing, and renewal that flow in the wake of following God's life-giving ways.

God really is not a spoil-sport. He's not out to take all the joy out of life with a lot of heavy demands and obligations, but to teach and train each of us in a life of joy and fulfillment. In this sense, God's approach is not unlike parents of very young children. Parents know from a vastly larger experience of life what will promote the health and welfare of their children. Children, needless to say, are not always thrilled about or can even comprehend the life-enhancing lessons their parents are trying to impart. Trust is essential. So, too, trust in God and in His love for us is an essential part of the process of learning the culture of the kingdom.

The "yoke" of God's new covenant in Christ is not a rash of laws and obligations, but first and foremost, a new relationship with God Himself – a yoke that is "easy" and "light" because it participates in the life of God Himself, filled with His love, and empowered by His Spirit.

There is more than a hint here of the promise enunciated in the prophet Jeremiah in which God urges the people to follow "the good way and walk in it and find rest for your souls." Jeremiah 6:16

But what is the nature of this "rest" that Jesus offers His disciples? Here, some of the assumptions we inherit from our culture can make it difficult to see just what Jesus is getting at.

For many of us in our work-oriented society, the notion of "rest" has to do primarily with "down time," with no longer being "on," with being able to "relax" and restore the energies depleted by work, by our obligations, and commonly enough, by our relationships with other people.

Often this notion of "rest" involves the abundant diversions modern society affords, evading the hassles of reality with a movie or a sports event, or, in these days, by simply tuning out the world in front of a computer screen or on social media.

While a little "time off" – "unstringing the guitar," as a friend of mine puts it, is clearly a requirement for a healthy life, the idea of rest as a solo pursuit, as something enjoyed in isolation from others or as a form of evasion is not at all what Scripture has in mind.

"Rest" in Scripture is many things – from simple cessation from labor to the messianic "rest" of the kingdom of God, when all of humanity's struggles are overcome, all aspirations met – but it is always seen in the context of relationships.

For many of us, keeping the Lord's Day brought this truth home. It certainly played that role in my life. More years ago now than I care to remember, I had been giving an all-day retreat for charismatic renewal leaders, on a Saturday. As the day wore on, I found myself looking forward with growing anticipation to the retreat's end and to a projected solo drive to the seaside to watch the sun set, followed by a quiet solitary dinner somewhere.

As I was planning my discreet escape, one of my colleagues reminded me that that very night I had scheduled the first-ever Lord's Day celebration at my single men's household. People were already there waiting for me.

Needless to say, this did not come as a welcome reminder. Gone was the promise of a quiet relaxed evening after an exhausting day. Instead, more duties and social obligations awaited me. I had to walk the block around my apartment several times in order to work off my "attitude" – one of considerable frustration and regret. Finally, I steeled myself as best I could to face the brothers gathered for the Lord's Day at home.

When I arrived, one of the brothers, aware of the long day I'd had, took my coat and ushered me into a chair. Dinner was already cooking on the stove. The table was set. Someone had taken the trouble to distribute all the pamphlets for the Lord's Day service. The guitarist was tuning up. Everything had been taken care of. I didn't need to supervise or organize anything.

When the time came for the meal to begin, I apologized to my housemates for my lack of energy. After teaching all day, I didn't feel up to much tonight, I told them.

"But you're home," someone replied. "We knew it would be a hard day for you. Relax, you're with us. Nobody expects you to perform."

As the evening wore on, I came to a major realization. I had been seeking "rest" in a quiet evening by myself, in isolation, but I had found it in the presence of my brothers.

That night I discovered – not that it's never OK to have a quiet dinner by yourself -- but that God's rest, genuine recreation, is to found in the midst of loving relationships. This realization is one of the keys to the Lord's Day.

One additional point: The frenetic pace of most contemporary lives, and the multi-tasking character of the world we live in, makes it harder for us to relax and simply be with other people – to "rest" with others.

I remember a situation years ago in which a well-meaning family member, with a background in planning recreational events for children, routinely overloaded Saturday family evenings with the family with planned activities, such as focused discussions around the dinner table, group games and required sing-a-longs. Such activities are fine, of course, and belong in the repertory of family-generated entertainment; but the need to over-organize an evening's recreation can also betray anxiety and an unwillingness to simply "be" with others, without an agenda, without a plan. The activities associated with the Lord's Day should have a relaxed, unregimented feel about them and it's perfectly fine if Saturday evenings or Sunday afternoons consist in a quiet unstructured enjoyment of the company of others.

In this, I am reminded of James Agee's famous poetic evocation of a 1915 summer night with the family on a Knoxville, Tennessee lawn:

"It has become that time of evening when people sit on their porches, rocking gently and talking gently and watching the street and the standing up into their sphere of possession of the trees, of birds hung havens, hangars. People go by; things go by. A horse, drawing a buggy, breaking his hollow iron music on the asphalt; a loud auto, a quiet auto; people in pairs, not in a hurry, scuffling, switching their weight of aestival [of or occurring in summer] body, talking causally. . . On the rough wet grass of the back yard my father and mother have spread quilts. We all lie there, my mother, my father, my uncle, my aunt, and I too am lying there. . .They are not talking much, and the talk is quiet, of nothing in particular, . . . of nothing at all."

Work and Rest

"*Labor is a craft, but perfect rest is an art.*" Heschel, **The Sabbath**

We noted in the chapter on the Lord's Day and the Eucharist that in the earliest centuries of Christianity the leisure associated with Sunday had more to do with participating in the Liturgy than in an express reference to Sabbath rest and the demands of the Third Commandment.

However, by AD 321, when the emperor Constantine issued his famous edict declaring Sunday a universal holiday, a day free from work and commerce, the theology of the Lord's Day had begun to absorb express elements of the biblical Sabbath, such as the notion of rest from labor and the acquisition of goods, into the culture of the feast, the feast of the "new creation in Christ."

As an early sermon urges:

"We have often said: 'This day [Lord's Day] is given to you for prayer and rest. This is the day that the Lord has made, let us rejoice and be glad in it."

And the Catechism amplifies:

"Just as God 'rested on the seventh day from all his work which he had done,' human life has a rhythm of work and rest. The institution of the Lord's Day helps everyone enjoy adequate rest and leisure to cultivate their familiar, *cultural, social, and religious lives. On Sundays and other holy days of obligation, the faithful are to refrain from engaging in work and activities that hinder the worship due to God, the joy proper to the Lord's Day, the performance of works of mercy, and the appropriate relaxation of mind and body."* CCC:2184-2185

Reflecting on the nature of "work" is one of the keys to understanding the Lord's Day "rest" commended by the Church. And here the Jewish Sabbath tradition can be helpful to us.

The Jewish philosopher Abraham Heschel has some trenchant (and vivid) things to say about the nature of "work" and its relationship to Sabbath rest:

"He who wants to enter the holiness of the day must first lay down the profanity of clattering commerce, of being yoked to toil. He must go away from the screech of dissonant days, from the nervousness and fury of acquisitiveness . . . He must say farewell to manual work and learn to understand that <u>the world has already been created and will survive without the help of man</u>. Six days a week he will wrestle with the world, wringing profit from the earth; on the Sabbath we especially care for the seed of eternity planted in the soul. The world has our hands, but our soul belongs to Someone Else. <u>Six days a week we seek to dominate the world; on the seventh day we try to dominate the self.</u>"

This quotation provides a key to the attitude to work that informs the Lord's Day. While labor is a blessing and has a dignity all its own, the focus of most labor has to do with demonstrating human mastery over nature, with "dominating the world," and is necessarily attached to the anxieties of making a living. It is from this labor, from the world of profit, ambition, and striving, that the Lord's Day offers a respite and a haven.

Catholic thought, while never as precise (or as far-reaching) as Jewish law on this matter, similarly identifies the "work" that should be put aside on the Lord's Day, in general, as the work one does for a living.

As a survey article published some years ago on evolving Catholic attitudes toward "servile work" on Sundays noted that

"... man is absorbed in the daily struggle for existence and thus distracted from the ultimate; and this preoccupation is interrupted by Sunday rest."

It is difficult, to say the least, to make hard and fast rules in this area. People's lives and family circumstances will always need to be taken into account in any attempt to implement a Lord's Day lifestyle. And in many cases, individuals may need to "ease" themselves into observance of the Lord's Day over time, making what adjustments they can to participate ever more fully in the day's promise of rest and peace.

But taking in the concept is the first step: that one of the freedoms the Lord's Day holds out to us is the freedom from a 24/7 world, in which the "job" has no borders, in which work never really ends — even in our minds — leaving little time for those on whose behalf we labor or for self-discovery and true recreation, for the care and feeding of the "seed of eternity planted in the soul."

Heschel, again:

"All week we may ponder and worry whether we are rich or poor, whether we succeed or fail in our occupations; whether we accomplish or fall short of reaching our goals. But who could feel distressed when gazing at spectral glimpses of eternity, except to feel startled at the vanity of being so distressed?"

One final (and quite contemporary) observation about the challenge of rest: I am referring to the habit of compulsively "checking" internet sources during the day, particularly when one is supposedly enjoying the benefits of Sunday rest. (I am indebted to an article Jeff Vogel wrote in a recent issue of *Christian Century* for "convicting" me about my own bad habits in this area.)

David Ulin, a prominent Los Angeles Times literary critic, has recently called attention to the phenomenon of "checking."

"I can check my email in an instant, and twenty, thirty times a day, I do. What am I looking for? Something, everything, a way of staying on top of the information . . . It doesn't matter. The looking is an end in itself."

Checking is typically brief – a quick glance to see if there are any new emails, if there is a new Facebook notification, the latest headlines. It's easy to rationalize – "I'm just checking!" Obviously, such habitual (even mindless) recourses to social media raise important issues in terms of the rest to which the Lord's Day invites us.

Vogel, in his piece, asks the important question: What are we looking for in such repeated glances over our shoulder? He suggests, provocatively, that, in addition to the simple desire to look, to know what's going on, is the active pursuit of interruption.

"What compels us to respond so suddenly to the sound a newly arriving email, the vibrations of a text, or the sight of another notification? It's often as if we were waiting for the disruption."

He compares this to the classic problem of "boredom" or *acedia* in prayer and other spiritual exercises and the contemporary need for and access to constant stimulation.

This is worth pointing out, not because social media are evil in themselves, but because the Lord's Day offers us a golden opportunity to examine and regulate our use of them – particularly when the motivation for "checking" may be restlessness with the "slow" pace of love, peace, relationships, and genuine spiritual progress.

Chapter Six

Leisure

"*Now, our hope is that the true sense of sacramental visibility in the celebration of the Christian* cultus *should become manifest to the extent needed for drawing the man in us, who is 'born to work', out of himself, and should draw him out of the toil and moil of every day into the sphere of unending holiday, and should draw him out of the narrow and confined sphere of work and labor into the heart and center of creation.*" Josef Pieper, **"Leisure: The Basis of Culture***"*

In the ancient world, leisure, far from being "spare time," was a highly prized commodity. It was an essential element in the "good life" – and it was more than that. The Greeks called it *schole* (from which we get the word "school"), which denotes the state of a person who belongs to himself, who is, in other words, a free man. The Greek word also suggests the way in which leisure should be employed: in study, learning, and the pursuit of wisdom – the free man in the ongoing search for moral and intellectual improvement. This was not only for its own sake, but so that he might grow in freedom and self-possession and be ever more enlightened in the performance of the responsibilities he had assumed in life.

The opposite of the free man, in the Greco-Roman order of things, was the slave, the one who had no leisure, no time for self-reflection, and whose life was marked by endless drudgery and labor.

In classic Jewish thought, the ideal life was seen as the scholar's life, in which the pursuit of wisdom was paramount. When the dairyman Tevye, in the popular musical *Fiddler on the Roof,* contemplates the blessings of wealth in the famous song "If I Were a Rich Man," he ends his catalog with

"*If I were rich,*

I'd have the time that I lack to sit in the synagogue and pray.

And discuss the holy books with the learned men several hours every day.

That would be the sweetest thing of all."

This traditional concept of leisure as the property of free persons or the wealthy and as time devoted to the pursuit of wisdom does not imply that leisure is only for intellectuals and scholars or people of means. But what it does point to is that leisure is not meant to be employed for the purposes of evasion. Leisure should allow a person to embrace, to savor his or her life, not avoid it through mindless distractions. And, clearly, it should afford a weekly opportunity to take stock of our lives and attitudes, to reflect on our behavior, and to regain our sense of priorities, to recall once more again what's really important in life.

This concept of leisure as an opportunity to grow in wisdom in the life of the virtues, what Robert Nozick made famous in the late 1980s as "the examined life" – is a far cry from the vision of leisure promoted in today's consumerist culture.

For many people today, the operational maxim is: we work hard and we play hard. But by "play", usually one of two things is meant.

"Play" is <u>diversion</u>, "taking my mind off things", usually in the form of the passive consumption of popular pre-packaged entertainment. While there is nothing wrong with going to the movies or revisiting your favorite episodic television series online, we need to be aware of the larger pattern: looking to passive, often isolated consumption of entertainment as a principal means of relieving the pressures of life and of work.

This issue also comes up if college or professional sports is the entertainment product being consumed. There can hardly be an objection to the notion of watching athletic excellence in action or following the exploits of one's favorite teams. But, again, it's the bigger picture that we need to pay attention to: Is the sports channel my default option when I'm not obliged to do something or be somewhere, whenever I have a little "free time"? Is it on all the time, the "background noise" to my family's life? Do I have to be yanked, grumbling, away from the screen when family needs conflict with my need to "disappear" into my own little world?

Needless to say, isolation is part of the problem, the desire to retreat from relationships and responsibilities into the illusory comforts of a manufactured world. That's even the case when a group of people cultivate a habit— habit being the operative word – of sitting passively in front of a screen, especially if weekends tend to be organized around such viewing.

Again, there's nothing wrong with sports and there's nothing, in essence, wrong with entertainment – the issue is how it's used in our lives -- whether we have fallen into patterns that misuse these cultural goods in order to evade responsibilities and the need to relate to people, or to provide a substitute for things that are missing in our lives. In the most serious cases, the need for diversion raises questions about whether, in effect, we are evading our own lives by living in someone else's digital one. As a friend of mine, teaching a seminar on so-called "media literacy," on learning to be intelligent and discerning about the uses of the media, told his audience: "The basic question that has to be answered is: What am I not doing, what am I not attending to, what am I not experiencing while I am doing this?"

A final point here: I suppose it will not come as a shock to anyone if I say that media emanating from the secular culture are not value neutral. For the most part, they are owned and operated by large corporate entities with their own financial and cultural agendas. Needless to say, the vision of relationships and society, the sense of priorities and the notions of what's important, let alone moral, do not, in most cases, support the vision of life we find in the Gospels.

If we wish to create and cultivate a distinctive Catholic life in our homes and families, then we cannot afford to let the "world" sabotage that process by allowing the secular culture, through the media, to form and shape our minds, our hearts, and our appetites. There are many good uses to which the media may be put, including those devoted to diversion and entertainment – but undiscerning use of the media, "having the television on all the time," or "scrolling on social media night and day" will have its effect on our ability to embrace the life that the Lord has for us.

Another mistake people can make about "play" is to embrace "leisure pursuits" that look a lot like work.

Sue, as the work week draws to a close, heads straight for the gym for her rock-climbing class in preparation for the Saturday rowing competition and the training for the half-marathon that will take up most of Sunday, a race that our high-achiever is determined to win this time. After all this physical and mental exertion, Sue finds that she just wants to be alone, to chill in the few hours of Sunday that are left. From time to time, she wonders why she doesn't have many friends.

Or: David and Sally enroll their three older boys in state championship soccer leagues, the activities of which come to dominate and fill the family's weekends to the exclusion of almost anything else. Sometimes the other not-so-athletic siblings wonder if they count.

Or: Sam, who works for an engineering firm, has ambitions to be a professional writer. The weekend gives him the leisure to pursue his dream. He never fails to attend the writing class given by a local professor after work on Friday and the writers' group that meets for breakfast on Saturday mornings. This gives him just enough time to do story research at the library before the Saturday evening reading at the local bookstore, which he organizes. He usually manages to get to Mass on Sunday, but rushes home to try to get a full day of work in on his newest projects and to plot out his submission strategy to local literary magazines before bed.

As with the discussion of media, there's nothing wrong with soccer leagues or with people who decide to train for athletic competitions or with the efforts of aspiring writers. These are all laudable and worthwhile pursuits. But they can have the effect of employing leisure for some fairly unleisurely ends. It is hard to avoid the impression that high-intensity weekend pursuits have the appearance and characteristics of work, of a second job, or an avocation, or a profession.

The problem, both philosophically and psychologically, is that in this use of leisure, leisure as another arena for high intensity effort and struggle, for "driven-ness" – <u>we never really stop working</u>.

The fact that for many of us, that may not seem like such a problem, shows us how far we are from living a balanced, thoughtful life, shaped by gratitude and freedom, and how close we may be to a kind of practical servitude to our ambitions (realistic and not so realistic), to other people's ambitions and to the daunting standards of success our culture imposes.

Spiritually, this is a vital and infrequently addressed area of concern: the place of work in our lives and the potentially inhibiting effect it can have on our ability to respond to God.

How many of you have heard the expression (or used it, for that matter) that "my work is my prayer"? As early as the 19th century, the English writer Carlyle proposed that to work means to pray and that all genuine work is religion, heralding the emergence of what Thomist philosopher Josef Pieper has dubbed "the modern cult of work," work as religion. Clearly, there are ways that one can be prayerful at work; but in its most extreme form, "my work is prayer," in practice, rationalizes the substitution of work for the demands of a life of prayer.

As Pieper wrote in a prophetic essay on leisure written more than fifty years ago:

"The original conception of leisure . . . has become unrecognizable in the world of planned diligence and 'total labor', and in order to gain a clear notion of leisure, we must begin by setting aside the prejudice . . . that comes from over-valuing the sphere of work. In his well-known study of capitalism, Max Weber quotes the saying that '<u>one does not work to live; one lives to work</u>,' which nowadays one no one has much difficulty in understanding: it expresses the current opinion."

The Lord's Day, with its promise of rest and true leisure, tends to highlight this issue, the place of work and achievement in our lives, and to help us to find our way out of the work-driven habits that inhibit so many of us from living in the freedom won for us by Christ, and from real relationships and real peace.

As I close this chapter, I am reminded of an old Ray Bradbury short story I read in high school, *"The Pedestrian,"* in which the story's subject, Leonard Mead, walks down a street in his neighborhood on a wintry November evening in the year 2053. He seems taken aback by the beauties of the crisp Arizona night and the thrill of his frequent nightly walks.

As he passes the homes of his neighbors, he peers into the shadows to see many of them glued to their giant TV screens, the houses dark and eerie.

He is alone as he hikes toward a new destination, only to find himself halted by a patrol car.

Although he protests that he has done nothing wrong, the officers detain him and eventually inform that they are taking him to a nearby psychiatric research facility "for regressive tendencies." His crime? Apparently, taking a walk, looking at the world on his own without recourse to the "viewing screens" that, conveniently for law enforcement, keep his other neighbors perpetually off the streets.

Beyond the broad satire of the 1950's and the birth of the television-dominated living room, Bradbury, of course, is saying something important in his brief tale. The pedestrian dares to see the world as it is. He dares to open himself to direct experience and to remove himself from the ubiquitous hold of vicarious pleasure and of a world mediated by others.

This can be one of the special revelations of the Lord's Day. In a world not far off, time-wise, from Bradbury's 2053, and closer to it in terms of media saturation than we might like to think, we dare to experience real life for ourselves. In turning down the media clamor, and freeing ourselves from the demands of hyper-activity, the Lord's Day gives us a chance to turn the volume up on life, to hear the children, to visit with neighbors, to take a walk with an ailing friend, to play a game in the backyard, to really listen in depth to someone's life story, to explore a topic of interest over coffee with someone knowledgeable, to sing, to play a piece on the piano, to have a leisurely conversation with your daughter about her college plans, to garden, to open a book you've been wanting to crack for years, to simply be aware of the real (not manufactured) sounds of the world around you, and, yes, to take a walk in the neighborhood just to see what you can see.

Chapter Seven

Joy

"Christianity is joy. . . . We Christians are not so accustomed to speak of joy, of happiness. I think we prefer to complain. . . Often Christians look as if they are [joining] a funeral procession rather than going to praise God. . . As the great Pope Paul VI said, You cannot advance the Gospel with sad, hopeless, discouraged Christians. . . Joy is the touchstone of a person's faith." Pope Francis, General Audience, May 31, 2013

"The Sabbath is no time for personal anxiety or care, for any activity that would dampen the spirit of joy. The Sabbath is no time to remember sins, to confess, to repent or even to pray for relief or anything we might need. It is a day of praise." Abraham Joshua Heschel

Friedrich Nietzsche, I think, would have agreed with the Pope's sentiment about joy. The German philosopher, no friend of Christianity, once famously wrote: "I might believe in the Redeemer if his followers looked more redeemed."

This is worth noting when we think about evangelization. Attracting people to Christianity is not principally a function of ideology or media savvy, still less of "salesmanship." It really has to do with the way we live in the world, with the witness of Catholic lives and Catholic culture, with the good life with which we are blessed, with all its struggles, because of Christ.

All of this reminds me of an incident that occurred not so long ago in my parish. I belong to an Eastern Catholic church in my hometown and anyone who's ever been present at an Eastern Catholic or Eastern Orthodox celebration of Pascha (or Easter) knows that it is not a sedate, meditative affair.

"Christ is risen!" rings out dozens of time during the course of the Easter Matins and Divine Liturgy, over-riding the choir as it chants the ecstatic verses the seventh-century poet St. John Damascene wrote for the feast:

"Today is the Day of the Resurrection: Let us be jubilant, O people, for this Passover is the Passover of the Lord, for Christ our God made us pass from death to life and from earth to heaven . . . Today let us celebrate the death of

Death and the overthrow of Hell [Hades] and the beginning of another life which is eternal . . . O faithful, come on this day of the Resurrection, let us drink the fruit of the New Vineyard, of the divine joy, of the kingdom of Christ!"

At the climax of the Matins service, the Easter sermon of St. John Chrysostom is read, one of the greatest homilies of all time, in some traditions to the vigorous shouts of the congregation:

" . . . *Come, you all, enter into the joy of your Lord. You the first and you the last, receive alike your reward; you rich and you poor, dance together; you sober and you who are weak, celebrate the day . . . The table is richly laden: enjoy its royal banquet. . . Let no one grieve over his poverty, for the universal kingdom has been revealed; let no one weep over his sins, for pardon has shone from the grave; let no one fear death, for the death of our Savior has set us free . . .O death, where is your sting? O Hades, where is your victory? Christ is risen and you are abolished, Christ is risen and the demons are cast down, Christ is risen and the angels rejoice, Christ is risen and life is freed!"*

In many parishes, this high-octane style of worship goes on into the early hours of the morning, after which an equally high-octane breakfast of sausage and other rich foods is served.

Some years ago, as the lined formed for breakfast in the parish courtyard after the long joyous services, some parishioners, in conversation, had already shifted the focus of their attention from "the joy of the Resurrection" to the unhappy state of their finances.

Observing the rapidity of this descent from celebrating the "death of Death" to bemoaning the rise of property taxes, several parishioners took matters into their own hands and started singing hearty renditions of the Pascha hymn while we all stood in line.

"Christ is risen from the dead, trampling down Death by death, and granting life to those in the tombs!"

To those eager to return to the familiar, to the recitation of worries and complaints, other parishioners greeted with good-natured insistence:

"Come on, Joe, Christ is risen!

It worked. The joy of Easter morning, the vision of "indestructible life" that lifts and enlightens our sorrows, lingered on a while longer.

But the event caused me to think about joy. What is the character of Christian joy? First of all, it isn't simply to be equated with an emotion like happiness or cheerfulness. It isn't a matter of one's disposition or personality type. In Scripture, joy is rooted in praise and thanksgiving. At the end of the Psalter (Psalms 148-150), the Psalmist calls on all creation, heaven and earth, to "praise the Lord":

"Praise God in his sanctuary;

Praise him in his mighty firmament!

Praise him for his mighty deeds;

Praise him according to his exceeding greatness!

Let everything that lives and that breathes

Praise the Lord!" Psalm 150

At the heart of Scripture's insistence on praising God is the recognition of reality – of the real world we all live in.

Some years ago, a new Catholic convert approached me about the predominant note of praise in Catholic worship. "Why does God need all that praise," she said. "Is He insecure?"

Trying to find a way to help her, I offered the perspective that praise and thanksgiving are necessary for us, not for God. He does not need our praise. It is we who need the language of praise and thanksgiving in order to appreciate the real situation we are in, to see our lives for what they really are – utterly dependent upon the grace of a loving God.

As Pope Francis said in the general audience address quoted above: "Without joy we Christians cannot become free; we become slaves to our sorrows. . .We gain joy through praise. In praising God, we come out of ourselves." Praise affirms that we and our problems are not the center of the universe, and that the redemption and freedom won for us by Christ surround us on every side – if we would only open our eyes.

In addition, the language of praise and thanksgiving prepares us for the life of heaven — basic training in the native language of the angels and saints, which is the language of praise.

"Then I looked, and I heard around the throne and the living creatures and the elders, the voice of many angels, numbering myriads of myriads and thousands of thousands, saying with a loud voice, 'Worthy is the Lamb who was slain, to receive power and wealth and wisdom and might and honor and glory and blessing!' And I heard every creature in heaven and on earth and under the earth and in the sea and all therein saying, 'To him who sits upon the throne and to the Lamb be blessing and honor and glory and might for ever and ever!' And the four living creatures said, 'Amen!' and the elders fell down and worshiped." Revelation 5:11-14

Since life with God is the purpose for which we humans were created, in a very real sense, we become ourselves most fully when we praise God. Joy is the natural offspring of the habit of praise. Joy is also a gift of the Holy Spirit. As Pope Francis affirmed in the address quoted above: "It is the Holy Spirit who gives us joy. It is the Spirit who guides us: He is the author of joy, the creator of joy. And this joy in the Holy Spirit gives us true Christian freedom."

For many Catholics, the most dramatic experience of this joy in the Holy Spirit often comes in the context of an explicit prayer for the "release" of the Holy Spirit. This prayer, familiar to those in the charismatic renewal, is often referred to as being "baptized in the Spirit" — a personal prayer asking that the power of the Holy Spirit we have already received in the Sacraments be released in our lives and relationships.

Some years ago, I witnessed a man praying for this "release in the Spirit" who had what initially seemed an odd reaction to the experience. He laughed — out loud and heartily. When asked later what had been going on, he said simply that he had never known the joy that overwhelmed him in that moment and that in the light of God's love, the endless worries that preoccupied him, the striving and struggle for the "good life" that sapped away all his time and energy seemed not only counter-productive, but ridiculous.

This "joy in the Holy Spirit" is not merely a matter of emotion or a one-time peak religious experience, but something the Holy Spirit wishes to build into our lives. Joy, after all, is one of the "fruits" or signs of the Holy Spirit that the Apostle Paul writes about in Galatians:

"But the fruit of the Holy Spirit is love, joy, peace, patience, kindness, goodness, faithfulness, gentleness, self-control." Galatians 5:22

Far beyond dramatic signs and wonders, these are the concrete manifestations of the work of the Holy Spirit in the lives of Christians, who strives day by day to form in each of us the character of Jesus. But, as we noted in the beginning of this chapter, there is a special connection between Christian joy and the Resurrection.

Hearkening back to my experience as an Eastern Catholic celebrating Pascha (Easter), one Easter, early in the morning, after services and as the festive breakfast was winding down, I wandered back into the still brilliantly lit church. The candles were lit, all the lights were on as they had been several hours earlier when we left the church for the blessing of Easter baskets and the meal. The open "royal doors" leading to the sanctuary caught my particular attention. In Slavic Eastern practice, the altar and sanctuary are screened from view most of the year by a tall iconostasis (or icon screen); but on Easter and the season that follows, the doors to the altar, normally shut and curtained off, stand wide open.

Alone in the church, I sat down on one of the chairs facing the sanctuary and looked intently through the open "royal doors." The deep meaning of this simple gesture began to dawn on me. In the Resurrection, as St. John Chrysostom preached, "Christ is risen and life is freed." The open doors were telling me that God's grace was open, available, unconditional, all-powerful, utterly undeterred by human sin and failure, offering a life without limits, a life in which history and time had been overcome, in which everything was possible.

Each year now, at Pascha, after the services, and when the festivities are winding down, I renew my once accidental custom and sit down before the open doors to the sanctuary, to taste once more, in silence, the freedom and the joy.

"Let no one grieve over his poverty, for the universal kingdom has been revealed; let no one weep over his sins, for pardon has shown from the grave;

let no one fear death, for the death of our savior has set us free." This taste of the reality of the Resurrection is at the heart of what the Lord's Day is all about.

One of the founders of City of Lord wrote recently:

"I think what impressed me most about those early experiences of the Lord's Day was the joy – the idea that Sunday, for Christians, was to be a day of joy, singing, and celebration, a weekly experience of the reality of the Resurrection. For me, I think, the Resurrection was more like an article of faith than an experience. Inauguration of the Lord's Day challenged me to put aside the troubles of the week, the stresses of work, and the worries about children, money, and the future that preoccupy most of us and give myself over – even for the day – to tasting the joy of Christ's victory over sin and death."

Oddly enough, over the years, I've found that one of the ways to foster that particular Lord's Day joy is through singing – through the use of table songs, songs sung around the family dinner table. The custom of singing table songs, short easy refrains that everyone knows, in the course of a long meal is a feature of the traditional Jewish Shabbat.

But we found the idea helpful, too, as a way of loosening up the atmosphere around the Lord's Day table and, in the best of circumstances, fostering a kind of liveliness, merriment, and cheer wholly appropriate to the day. Over time, we developed and assembled a group of table songs, some Christian adaptations of Shabbat songs, others selected out of our own repertoire of praise songs and choruses from hymns.

Table-singing or family singing, of course, used to be a common pastime, especially on Sundays and family occasions. It remains a very effective way to create unity and evoke an atmosphere and also provide a simple form of self-generated family entertainment. But there are a number of things to keep in mind:

- The songs selected as table songs, for the most part, should be short and memorable, as simple as a refrain; something everyone can sing.

- The songs should be joyful and spirited, appropriate to the occasion.

- Some of the songs might be ones that are only sung on Lord's Days, songs people look forward to singing and symbolize the special atmosphere of the day.

- While booklets of Lord's Day songs might be put together as an aid or for guests, it's important that the process of singing is not cumbersome or that people at the table have their heads buried in the music.

This last point is especially important. Ideally, there should be a lot of good cheer around the Lord's Day table. The inauguration of the Lord's Day should be a life-giving and enjoyable experience – not a solemn duty to be gotten through. Nothing helps life happen at the table like spirited singing. And nothing "kills" the atmosphere around the table quite as effectively as leaders who insist on "over-organizing" the celebration. The Lord's Day should not be "work" – even for those who have the responsibility to lead them. The practical effectiveness of the Lord's Day – its promise of "rest" -- depends on a spirit of freedom and informality.

In order to foster this essential "informality," my household had a rule that anyone at the table could start a song. Further, that anyone could start a song at any time! I realize that this may not be an approach that every family or household may be willing to risk, or should risk, for that matter. But what the "when-in-doubt-break-into-song" rule ensured was not only a very lively evening, but one which I, the table leader, was strongly discouraged from getting overly serious over dinner, or worse yet, long-winded!

Chapter Eight

Peace

Many years ago, a close friend's father, who came originally from Lebanon, told this fascinating story. (He had many of them.) A young Christian man traveling in the Mount Lebanon area near Druze villages (the Druze follow a highly individual eclectic and heterodox version of Shi'a Islam) was attacked without provocation by a Druze man on the road. In defending himself, he killed the Druze attacker. Making his way into a nearby village, he sought shelter for the night. The town's most distinguished citizen, a Druze noble, welcomed him in peace, offered him shelter for the night and insisted that he join him for the evening meal. As the evening wore on, and reports of a body found on the road drifted in, the atmosphere became increasingly tense. Eventually, the body was identified as the nobleman's son and suspicions were aroused that this stranger might be implicated in the killing. Sensing the danger, the Christian told his host what had happened on the road.

Silencing the voices of his sons who cried for revenge, the Druze nobleman indicated to his guest that the son he had accidentally killed had had a history of mental instability and violent behavior. Further, he indicated to the thoroughly frightened stranger that because he had given him the greeting of peace and had shared his meal with him, no harm would (or could) come to him while he remained under his roof.

Despite the tragedy that had befallen him, the host, in effect, recognized that he had made a covenant of peace with his guest and that this peace superseded any urge for retribution.

When his sons had gone, the old man advised the young Christian to leave the house before dawn and counseled him about the safest routes to take out of the village. The young man Christian made his escape and, luckily, found his way back to the safety of his own town.

What this story illustrates is an important lesson about the biblical notion of peace.

Peace (*shalom*, in Hebrew) is more than the mere absence of war and conflict. It is a positive commitment to the well-being of others, to their safety, health, and prosperity.

Far from something based on mood or disposition, "peace," as the Lebanon story exemplifies, is covenantal. Once entered into with another person or persons, it commits the peace-maker to a code of behavior that ensures the health and safety and security of those to whom "peace" has been given.

There is an "earthy" quality to Scripture's concept of peace: peace is the well-being of daily life, good health, security, and harmony in the community, between neighbors and with nature.

When Joseph in Egypt asks his brothers about the well-being of Jacob, their common father, he asks (literally):

"Is he in <u>peace (shalom)</u>?" By which, of course, he means is their father in good health (Genesis 43:27).

The Hebrew Scriptures have this same concrete quality when they reference what it means for God to give "peace."

"*Trust in the Lord and do good; so you will dwell in the land and enjoy security [peace]. Take delight in the Lord, and he will give you the desires of your heart.*" Psalm 37:4

"*There are many who say, 'O that we might see some good! Lift up the light of thy countenance, O Lord!' Thou hast put more joy in my heart that they have when their grain and wine abound. <u>In peace I will both lie down and sleep; for thou alone, O Lord, makest me dwell in safety.</u>*" Psalm 4:6-8

And the prophet Ezekiel, looking forward to Israel's restoration, sees it as the renewal of a covenant of peace:

"*I will make with them a covenant of peace and banish wild beasts from the land, so that they may dwell securely in the wilderness and sleep in the woods. And I will make them and the places round about my hill a blessing; and I will send down the showers in their season; they shall be showers of blessing. And the trees of the field shall yield their fruit and the earth shall yield its increase, and they shall be secure in their land . . . They shall no more be a prey to the nations, nor shall the beasts of the land devour them; they shall dwell securely, and none shall make them afraid."* Ezekiel 34:25-28

In the New Testament, the concept of "peace" is broadened but it still does not lose this "concrete" behavioral and social dimension.

Through His sacrifice, death and Resurrection, Jesus, as Paul proclaims in Ephesians, has broken down the divisions of human history and created the real basis for peace and reconciliation among men:

"But now in Christ Jesus, you who were far off [Gentiles] have been brought near in the blood of Christ. For he is our peace, who has made us both [Jews and Gentiles] one and has broken down the wall of hostility . . . that he might create in himself one new man in place of the two, so making peace, and might reconcile us both to God in one body through the cross, thereby bringing the hostility to an end . . . So then you [Gentiles] are no longer strangers and sojourners, but you are fellow citizens with the saints and members of the household of God." Ephesians 2:13-19

The peace that Jesus comes to bring is not merely an individual blessing or even the social blessing of a good and tranquil life the Hebrew Scriptures celebrate; it is the basis of universal unity culminating in the body of Christ -- transcending cultural and ethnic differences, even the division of heaven and earth -- and the instrument of reconciliation and healing in the world.

"For in him all the fullness of God was pleased to dwell, and through him to reconcile to himself all things, whether on earth or in heaven, making peace by the blood of his cross." Colossians 1:19-20

Peace Equals Right Relations

The thing to notice about all these Scriptural passages: In different ways, they emphasize peace in the context of <u>relationships</u> – peace as covenantal bond, peace as security brought about by good harmonious relations, health as the blessing secured by the care and loyalty of others, peace as concord between humanity and nature.

To attempt a definition: peace in Scripture is <u>right relations</u> – it is *shalom*. Peace, in the biblical sense, always and by its very nature involves others; <u>one only has it (peace) when one has it with other people</u>. In this sense, peace is close to justice, as in just relations – people behaving toward one another according to God's standards and with the respect due to others made in the image and likeness of God. The <u>effects</u> of peace may, indeed, be a personal sense of well-being, happiness, tranquility. But these, in a sense, are the happy by-products of good, just, and loyal and life-giving relationships.

This is an important point – particularly in today's cultural climate. It's common nowadays to associate peace almost exclusively with "feelings" – I'm at peace when I'm feeling peaceful. Often enough, we associate feelings of peace not with relationships, but with <u>getting away from them</u>, with isolation.

"I'll feel better about things once I get on the road and it's just me and the radio."

"I can't wait to get away for a few days and find a little peace and quiet."

While there's nothing wrong with a weekend away to rest and refresh oneself, or with a walk in the park to "hear yourself think" – such things, in fact, are essential to good psychological health -- our culture has a tendency to "privilege" feelings – to make how one feels at any given moment the measure of what's true, and, often, the determining factor in what we do or don't do.

"I used to feel a sense of peace when I came to church, but that's gone now. I wonder sometimes why I still go to church."

We sometimes go so far as to imagine that to do something without having the requisite emotions at the time is somehow false or "inauthentic."

While emotions are a profound part of what makes us human, they are not, in a Christian sense, the motivating agent of our actions. Emotions can enrich our actions, emotions can bolster them – but they were never intended to determine them. <u>God's call to love and serve is the motivation for Christian action</u>. A Christian hardly needs to wait for an overpowering emotion in order to serve the elderly neighbor down the block, or, conversely, to feel that his or her service to the food pantry is wanting or inauthentic because it doesn't evoke powerful feelings.

As with our reflections on "rest," the Lord's Day can provide us with opportunities to discover that real peace is to be found, not in isolation from others, but in their midst – a peace we don't (and can't) engineer for ourselves, but which we find only in the presence of the Lord and His people.

"I will hear what the Lord God has to say, a voice that speaks of peace, peace for his people and his friends and those who turn to him in their hearts. His help is near for those who fear him and his glory will dwell in our land. Mercy and faithfulness have met; justice and peace have embraced. Faithfulness shall spring from the earth and justice look down from heaven. The Lord will make us prosper and our earth shall yield its fruit. Justice shall march before him and peace shall follow his steps." Psalm 84:9-14

The Art of Contentment

"The Christian community has not been given to us by God for us to be continually taking its temperature. The more thankfully we daily receive what is given to us, the more assuredly and consistently will the community increase and grow from day to day, as God wishes. . . Christian community is not an idea we have to realize, but rather a reality created by God in Christ in which we may participate." Dietrich Bonhoeffer, **Life Together**

Learning to be content with relationships as they are – better yet, following Bonhoeffer's language, to "receive them as they are" -- is an aspect of peace that can provide a special challenge (as well as an opportunity) in the context of the Lord's Day.

What I do mean by "learning to be content" with things as they are? Working to improve situations, attitudes, correcting faults, disciplining wrongdoing – all these are part and parcel of week-day striving for Catholic parents, priests, and pastoral leaders. While I'm certainly not suggesting that parents can take a day off from parenting or that clear wrongdoing can be piously disregarded on Sundays, what I am saying is that the peace of the Lord's Day should involve a certain weekly respite from the urge to improve people, to have everything just so, to make everyone behave the way I wish they would.

How many Lord's Day family dinners have I sat through in which fathers conducted the meal in the "drill sergeant" manner – "We will now turn to page 23 in the Lord's Day book – and that means you, too, Tim!" – or where the urge to improve table manners or to express impatience with the difficulty "Jane" always has "getting to the point" when she shares about her week are indulged.

Part of the art of the Lord's Day – and it is a learned behavior – is growing in our capacity to accept people in our parishes, our families, our convents, our communities as they are – to be at peace with them – to accept the fact that they don't always speak or behave the way we might wish them to, or even the way we know they should. This is not to say that we look the other way if clear wrongdoing or injustice should occur, but that we learn to be patient with each other's idiosyncrasies and character flaws. On this day, in which we celebrate Christ's victory over all limitations, even our own, we are grateful for the progress we and our families have made in living the Christian life and lay down the burden of having to ensure that everyone reaches the perfection we have in mind.

Again, this is not to say that table leaders cannot gently steer an overly talkative guest into "wrapping it up" or imposing a measure of good order on the proceedings. But it should be done in the peace and joy of the Lord's Day – abandoning, for the moment, our own agendas for improvement, our own images of what people should be like, along with our desires to control and manage others.

For pastoral leaders, this is often a daunting proposition – to be content, even for a scant twenty-four hours, with what "is" rather than to continue the struggle for what might or should be. But without this "art of contentment", peace will often elude the very people leading the Lord's Day endeavor. And, often enough, in the willingness to listen and relax in the presence of others, one finds wisdom and insight into the people we care for (and about) that had entirely escaped us.

Chapter Nine

Mercy

"It is mercy (steadfast love) that I desire and not sacrifice, the knowledge of God rather than burnt offerings." Hosea 6:6

"The Eucharist commits us to the poor. To receive in truth the Body and Blood of Christ given up for us, we must recognize Christ in the poorest, His brethren. CCC:1397

In this striking biblical passage from Hosea, we have a particularly vivid affirmation of what we might well call the *logic* of the Eucharist. (By the way, the biblical prophet Hosea is not saying that God is indifferent to sacrifice and worship. Later in chapter 9:4, Hosea implies that the deprivation of sacrifice is a form of <u>divine punishment.</u>) What the prophet <u>is</u> saying is that the purpose of worship is not to shield us, even temporarily, from the demands of the world, to create a kind of "spiritual cocoon," but, rather to prepare and equip us go back out into it, empowered by the Spirit, as agents of God's mercy and compassion.

In liturgical scholar Louis Bouyer's memorable words:

"The world of the sacraments, the world into which the liturgy introduces us, is not a world in its own right, standing aloof from the world of ordinary living. It is rather the <u>meeting-point of the world of the Resurrection with this very world of ours</u> in which we must live, suffer, and die. And this fact implies that liturgical life, far from taking us out of real life, far from making us indifferent to or uninterested in real life, on the contrary positively sends us back into it in order to carry out fully in it the Mystery which has come to us through the sacraments."

No one had a better grasp of the radical character of this Eucharistic logic than did the great fourth-century Antiochian preacher John Chrysostom. As patriarch of Constantinople, he got himself into serious trouble with the political elite more than once by insisting on the rights of the poor and on the innate connection between worshipping Jesus in the Eucharist and serving the needs of the poor, the sick, and the destitute.

Two remarkable, and challenging, passages from his sermons:

"Do you wish to honor Christ's body? Do not neglect him then when he is naked; do not, while you honor him here with silken garments, neglect him perishing outside of cold and nakedness. For he that said, 'This is my body,' and by his word confirmed the fact, also said: 'You saw me hungry and you did not feed me' and 'whatever you did for the least of these, you did for me.' Apply this also to Christ when he comes along the roads as a pilgrim, looking for shelter. You do not receive him as your guest, but you decorate the floors and walls and capitals [of your churches]. Once again, I am not forbidding you to supply such adornments: I am urging you to provide these other things as well, and, indeed, to provide them first. . . . Do not therefore adorn the church and neglect your afflicted brother, for he is the most precious temple of all."

"You indeed honor this altar because it receives Christ's body, but him that is himself the body of Christ you treat with contempt, and when he is perishing, ignore. This altar you see around you everywhere, in lanes and marketplaces, and you may sacrifice upon it every hour, for on this altar, too, sacrifice is performed . . . When, then, you see a poor believer, think that you behold an altar; when you see a beggar, do not merely refrain from insulting him, reverence him."

More than seventeen hundred years later, these words still startle and confront us.

The Catechism, too, stresses this notion that the works of mercy constitute a key element in the observance of the Lord's Day.

"On Sundays . . . the faithful are to refrain from engaging in work or activities that hinder the worship owed to God, the joy proper to the Lord's Day, <u>the performance of the works of mercy</u>, and the appropriate relaxation of mind and body[1] *. . . Sunday is traditionally consecrated by Christian piety to good works and humble service of the sick, the infirm, the elderly."* CCC:2185-2186

The concept that Sundays, particularly Sunday afternoons, might be devoted to paying visits to the sick, to shut-ins, elderly relatives, the dying would not have seemed strange to Catholics a few generations ago. But this essential element in Lord's Day culture may need renewal in our times. And not only in the narrow sense of reviving the customs of the recent past: visiting relatives and friends, for example, but as something to be developed and expanded as an expression of Christian witness and as an integral part of Lord's Day culture.

We're not talking here about a dutiful prayer or two for the sick, but something far more creative and demanding: a work of Christian moral imagination. What would our lives be like, what would the lives of others be like, if we used our imaginations in loving others, in showing mercy, and in expressing solidarity with the poor?

I know a deacon who spends each Sunday afternoon, after brunch with his family, ministering to prisoners at a facility in his hometown. He's not able to do much in the maximum security environment in which he works; all he's allowed to do is press his hands on the glass, often meeting the hands of prisoners on the other side. But parolees have told him many years later how powerful that wordless prayer, that "touchless" touch was each week. What a sign of God's mercy it was and how it had saved them from despair.

Some years ago, members of my parish routinely paid calls on a Catholic AIDS hospice most Sundays and holidays. They would pray with the men, women, and children there, often forming bonds that opened up possibilities for witness and spiritual support. For years our parish choir sang carols at Christmas for the patients, and a small group ministered in a special way to the dying.

A group of Protestant ministers in San Francisco made news recently by going into so-called "flop houses" in the inner city to arrange memorial services for the many "nameless" poor who had died there. "No one should die and be forgotten," they said as they worked with locals to restore life stories and visibility to these invisible souls.

Recently, I myself had an experience of how deeply meaningful Sunday can be as a day devoted not only to rest and family, but to bringing God's mercy and comfort to others.

I serve as the choir director at my parish. One of my singers had been diagnosed with cancer, and, while she had "soldiered on" for many months, was finally bedridden with the debilitating effects of her disease. Her husband is also a member of my choir and, after Sunday services, fellow choir members piled into cars and paid her an afternoon visit.

Expecting that her condition would permit only a short stay, we found her dressed, eager to greet us, and ready to regale us with vivid tales of hospital misadventures and the antics of the neurotic family cats. After a while, we handed her a choir book and she followed along as we sang familiar and well-loved liturgical pieces. A few simple refreshments were served and as she began to tire, we prayed together, and took our leave. By now, it was late in the day, and what we had imagined would be a quick house call had lengthened into hours of sharing, song, prayer and encouragement.

"Now that's a way to spend a Sunday afternoon," one of the choir members said approvingly as we made our way to the cars.

A final note: One of the side benefits of investing time in performing acts of kindness and mercy, especially in the context of the Lord's Day celebrations, is that it provides an opportunity to involve children in regular visits to the sick, the needy, and the dying.

In the past, it would have been considered natural in most cultures for children to be active participants in caring for sick and dying relatives and in providing for the poor. We need only think about the once-common practice of gathering whole families in the room of a dying relative to witness the loved one's passing.

Our consumerist society, however, with its preoccupation with youthfulness and health, has largely walled-off the world of the needy and the sick. These are addressed in mostly professional contexts and in institutions. Often enough, nowadays, children from more affluent families are effectively shielded from much personal contact with difficult realities: serious illness, need, poverty, and death. This leaves many young people today ill-equipped emotionally and spiritually to deal with realities that sooner or later must touch us all, and that have a claim on our love, courage, and compassion.

Building care for others into the celebratory activities of the Lord's Day not only enriches the meaning of leisure, but can also enable family members, on a regular basis, to come to terms with the realities of life, thereby growing in faith, sober awareness, and the capacity to give love and care in difficult and demanding circumstances.

Chapter Ten

The Eighth Day

"If then you have been raised with Christ, seek the things that are above, where Christ is, seated at the right hand of God. Set your minds on things above not on things that are on earth. For you have died, and your life is hidden with Christ in God. When Christ who is our life appears, then you also will appear with him in glory." Colossians 3:1-4

"Jesus rose from the dead 'on the first day of the week.' Because it is the 'first day,' the day of Christ's Resurrection recalls the first creation. Because it is the 'eighth day' following the Sabbath, it symbolizes the new creation ushered in by Christ's Resurrection. For Christians, it has become the first of all days, the first of all feasts, the Lord's Day – Sunday: We all gather on the day of the sun, for it is the first day [after the Jewish Sabbath, but also the first day] when God, separating matter from darkness, made the world; and on this same day Jesus Christ our Savior rose from the dead." CCC:2174, quoting St. Justin Martyr

For the early Church, Sunday was meant to be far more than a mere commemoration of the Resurrection of Jesus. It was meant to be a living experience of the kingdom of God, opened to us in the victory of Jesus over sin and death, and made present to us now in the power of the Holy Spirit.

The Fathers of the Church, the great Christian theologians of the first centuries, highlighted this view of Sunday as an anticipation of heaven by calling it "the eighth day." It is important for us to take this patristic notion seriously, as the Catechism does, because it makes it clear to us that Sunday is meant to be more than simply a "family day," as good as that is, or as a day of relaxation and recreation without deeper significance.

For the Fathers, Sunday was not only the weekly memorial to the Resurrection, and, therefore, the setting for the celebration of the Eucharist, it was also the image, or icon of the age to come. As the late Orthodox theologian Father Alexander Schmemann explains:

"Christ rose not on the Sabbath, but on the first day of the week. The Sabbath was the day of His rest, His 'en-sabbathment' in the tomb. But the new

life, the life which had begun to shine out of the tomb, . . . this was the first day, the beginning of the new life over which death has no dominion. . . This day which concludes the history of salvation, the day of victory over the forces of evil is also the eighth day, since it is the beginning of a new [age]."

As St. Basil the Great amplifies:

"The Lord's Day is great and glorious. The Scriptures knows this day without evening, having no other day, a day without end; the Psalmist called it the eighth day, since it is outside of time measured in weeks."

The notion is attested in some of the oldest Christian sources, such as the (non-canonical) Epistle of Barnabas, dating from the early 2nd century:

"It is not your Sabbaths that I love, but the one I have made, wherein putting an end to the universe, I shall inaugurate a new world. This is why we celebrate with joy the eighth day on which Jesus rose again."

Or St. Hilary of Poitiers:

"Although the name and observance of the Sabbath has been established for the seventh day, it is the eighth, which is also the first, that we ourselves celebrate, and this is the feast of the perfect Sabbath."

While the patristic preoccupation in symbols and symbolic analysis can sometimes puzzle us, there is something vital and necessary in this mystical notion of the "eighth day."

For the Fathers, the importance of this "eternal" dimension of the Lord's Day is to apply the power and vision of the Resurrection to the lives of Christians in the here and now, to foster an authentic love and expectation of the heavenly life to come – an appetite for heaven -- and to prevent Christians from losing their sense of perspective by allowing their lives to be swallowed up in worldly affairs and the things of earth.

This orientation toward eternity, toward the vision of the world to come, can run up against some cultural and even religious barriers these days. Outside of funeral Masses, one may not hear much about heaven, the love of heaven, or the world to come, in contemporary Catholic piety. In part, this may be due to the sentimental approaches of the past, even the recent past, in which the grandeur and awesomeness of the biblical vision of the worshiping cosmos assembled in the presence of God is largely reduced to sentimental imagery — to cuddly angels with harps. In addition, a consumerist mindset firmly fixed on the here and now certainly plays a role in "agnostic" or hazy attitudes about the life to come one encounters.

But as Heschel sagely observes:

"Unless one learns how to relish the taste of Sabbath while still in this world, unless one is initiated in the appreciation of eternal life, one will be unable to enjoy the taste of eternity in the world to come. Sad is the lot of him who arrives inexperienced and when led to heaven has no power to perceive the beauty."

The Lord's Day, in this sense, is meant to be an anticipation of heaven, a taste of the world to come, basic training, if you will, in the eternal celebration of the angels and saints. This involves a great deal more than popular conceptions of heaven based on puffy clouds with saints. or even, in the first case, with popular culture's eschatological reunions with loved ones.

For the New Testament, the central reality of Heaven is <u>life with God.</u>

"Beloved, we are God's children now; <u>it does not yet appear what we shall be, but we know that when he appears, we shall be like him, for we shall see him as he really is.</u>" 1 John 3:2

"For now we see in a mirror dimly, but then <u>face to face</u>. Now I know in part, then I shall know [God] as fully as I am known [by God]." 1 Corinthians 13:12

"There shall no more be anything accursed, but the throne of God and the Lamb shall be in it [the new Jerusalem] and his servants shall worship him; <u>they shall see his face</u>, and his name shall be on their foreheads. And night shall be no more; they need no light or lamp or sun, for the Lord God will be their light, and they shall reign for ever and ever." Revelation 22:3-5

While the fullness of this "knowledge of God" will only be possible in eternity, when the limitations of earth and time have been removed, God's life, this same life, is available to us now in the sacraments and in the manifold ways God comes to us in our lives.

We are already participating, "imperfectly" as Paul says in First Corinthians, in the life of heaven, a life with God to which we are being drawn – and, in a fundamental sense, for which we are being prepared.

This fact has real implications for the way we think and for the priorities we establish in our lives. As Paul urges in the Letter to the Colossians:

"If then you have been raised with Christ, seek the things that are above, where Christ is, seated at the right hand of God. Set your minds on things that are above, not on things that are on earth. For you have died and your life is hid with Christ in God. When Christ who is our life appears, then you also will appear with him in glory." Colossians 3:1-4

This is an incomparably rich passage, but for our purposes, perhaps these three points are worth underlining:

Through Christ, we really do have access to the life and the perspective of eternity ("where Christ is").

This truth came alive for me when, as a young man, I visited an Eastern Catholic church for the first time. (I was not a Catholic – yet.) I was given a brief tour inside the church by a kindly parishioner – the dome representing the heavens, the icons symbolizing the "great cloud of witnesses," the angels and saints who surround us as we pray (Hebrews 12:1), the sanctuary with its sense of the mysterious hiddenness of God. I came to realize that we never pray alone – that through the power of the Holy Spirit, we are always positioned mystically in the court of heaven, before the Christ who will judge us, in the midst of the great multitudes of all ages who worship before the throne of God.

The passage doesn't imply that we ignore the things of earth or that we neglect our earthly responsibilities, but that we "set our minds," that is, allow our minds to be informed by the perspective of eternity and to see, judge, use, and evaluate the things of this world in its light.

This eternal perspective also involves the difficult truth that death and, through it, our participation in the mystery of Christ's Passion must be at the center of our consciousness – not on the periphery. Death comes, too often, for modern people as the unwelcome, unanticipated intruder into our dreams of retirement, not the daily life compass it is meant to be, orienting us in our daily choices, and awakening us to the beauty of every moment, to gratitude.

This awareness of eternity and the reality of death, far from being a grim or morbid preoccupation, manifests itself in the celebration of life. Mozart once confessed in a letter that the awareness of death, the beauty and fragility of life, accompanied him every day and was the paradoxical source of his creativity. It should not surprise us, then, that Mozart's music is alive with joy.

To say the least, then, the mentality Paul's Letter to the Colossians describes calls for courage, tough-mindedness and clarity. It is not an invitation to otherworldliness. The Anglican writer Harry Blamires puts it like this:

"A prime mark of the Christian mind is that it cultivates the eternal perspective. That is to say, it looks beyond this life to another one. It is supernaturally oriented and brings to bear upon earthly considerations the fact of Heaven and the fact of Hell . . . The Christian sees human life and human history held in the hands of God. It sees the whole universe sustained by His power and His love. It sees the natural order as dependent on the supernatural order, time as contained within eternity. It sees this life as an inconclusive experience, preparing us for another."

The Lord's Day can play a role in fostering such an eternal perspective in our families, in enhancing the experience of Sunday as the "eighth day."

First of all, the Lord's Day, centered on the Eucharist, and amplified in the domestic celebrations of the family, is itself an image of the kingdom. We have only to think of Jesus' parable of the wedding feast (Matthew 22:1-14) where the kingdom is compared with a family banquet or the vision of heaven in Revelation 19:9 as the marriage supper of the Lamb. The readings, prayers, and songs appropriate to the Lord's Day all serve to evoke these realities.

Secondly, in the Eucharist we receive each Sunday, we partake of the bread (the food) of heaven. As the Catechism affirms:

"In an ancient prayer the Church acclaims the mystery of the Eucharist: 'O sacred banquet in which Christ is received as food, the memory of the Passion is renewed, the soul is filled with grace and a pledge of the life to come is given to us.' . . . If by our communion at the altar we are filled 'with every

heavenly blessing and grace,' then the Eucharist is also an anticipation of the heavenly glory." CCC:1402

The focus of the Lord's Day on the Resurrection also offers us a weekly opportunity to remember that the victory over sin and death has already been won in Christ. We can live in the light of that victory, and remove from our minds and hearts and *conversations* – if only for a day – the cares and worries and frustrations that preoccupy us, and narrow our perspective the rest of the week.

This is true even in situations, perhaps especially in situations where a death in the family has occurred, where bereavement is still keen. As with all good community rituals, the Lord's Day, perhaps in a mellower key, can help steady people in the midst of the helplessness and grief, easing the isolation, and placing the loss in the merciful light of God's victory over death.

Finally, the Lord's Day can help us appropriate the vision of the "eighth day" because the culture of the Lord's Day is a culture of beauty, a beauty shaped by the intersection of this world and the world to come. Motivated by the vision of heaven, the Lord's Day invites us to live beautifully in this world – to use with thanksgiving all the good things God has placed in our lives: worship, food, drink, song, companionship, family, recreation, nature. In the shadow of the rest of God, we are invited to enjoy our lives in this world, to love, savor, and embrace them.

This insight is behind the Jewish notion that on Shabbat every man, even the most destitute, is a king. The stories of the Yiddish writer Scholem Aleichem are full of such characters who gather whatever meager means they have at their disposal – a Sabbath loaf given by the baker, a bit of dried fish saved for the occasion – and celebrate, clothing themselves, despite their poverty, in the dignity of the day.

This is a radical insight, the Lord's Day's invitation to <u>love our own lives</u> and the people who inhabit them; but it is an essential part of what the Lord's Day is meant to do and to foster. It's easy in our culture of constant acquisition and striving to curse ourselves, in effect, for not being someone else, for not having someone else's life or good fortune. The Lord's Day is intended to be much more than a simple corrective to such tendencies: to restore a little balance, to help us arrive at some kind of acceptance. The Lord's Day, in fact, is about creating a larger openness to life, in this world and beyond this world: to enable us, by tasting the life of God, by living a little on this day the way we will on That Day, to grow ever more fully, week by week, day by day, in our capacity to live, to see, to hear, to love and to praise.

"For this reason I bow my knees before the Father, from whom every family in heaven and on earth is named, that according to the riches of his glory he may grant you to be strengthened with power through his Spirit in the inner man, and that Christ may dwell in your hearts through faith; that you, being rooted and grounded in love may have power to comprehend with all the saints what is the breadth and length and height and depth, and to know the love of Christ which surpasses knowledge, that you may be filled with all the fullness of God." Ephesians 3:14-19

PART THREE: AFTERWORD

Chapter Eleven

The Lord's Day in a Post-Christian World

"A faith which does not become a culture is a faith not fully received, not thoroughly thought through, not fully lived out." Pope Saint John Paul II

In the 1970s, during the years when many Catholic charismatic communities were first forming, I think it's safe to say that there were two main motivating factors behind the trend to build community:

The sense of God's call. The emphasis of the charismatic renewal on commitment to the person of Jesus and openness to the gifts of the Holy Spirit, given for sake of the Church, brought people together around a desire to pursue lives of holiness and service. But that call did not stop with support and fellowship. Early on, people sensed that God was calling communities together in order to equip them to serve His people and to do frontline service in the work of the kingdom. This service dimension – that the gifts that communities have received from God belong, by right, to the whole Church – has been reinforced by the exhortations of recent popes, particularly Pope Saint John Paul II and Pope Francis.

The challenges emanating from an increasingly secularized culture. One of the chief insights that drove the move to build communities in the charismatic renewal centered on the recognition that major cultural supports of Christianity – from stable neighborhoods to family support systems – had weakened if not eroded entirely in America's postwar "mobile work force"-style society. This structural deficit was compounded by the challenges posed by a culture that was actively abandoning its moorings in Judeo-Christian values, intent on its pursuit of the consumerist good life and the ideals of radical individualism, the cult of what some cultural commentators have aptly called the "imperial self." Isolated Christians in a post-Christian world, it was clear, would find it increasingly difficult to live a full life of faith. While lay communities and associations would provide a support system for some, the main task, it seemed to us, was to help revivify the domestic church – the

Catholic marriage, Catholic family and family life – and to foster the development of a Catholic spiritual culture in parishes, a basic spiritual culture built on honor, gratitude, and covenant love – learning to be brothers and sisters in the Lord - that would help support, sustain, and strengthen our common faith and witness in the world.

If anything, the situation is even clearer today than it was in 1975. The choices are starker and the consequences of indifference more evident than ever.

By the beginning of the twenty-first century, the radical structural deficits, the lack of natural support systems for Christian life, were exacerbated by further erosion, and rejection in some quarters of even remnant Judeo-Christian values in the broader culture and by an aggressive impulse to marginalize the Church and its influence on public life. These trends grow more evident and, if anything, more pervasive as time goes on.

This has made it even harder than it was forty years ago to live an effective Christian life based on the old assumptions of shared cultural values, relying on the secular culture's largely benign, permissive view of faith. While not abandoning the call to engage the larger culture with the message of the Gospel, we must also take steps to attend to the state of our own spiritual infrastructure, too, and not only as a defensive measure, to protect ourselves and our values, but as an offensive, even missionary one: to incarnate the Gospel and its witness of love in a genuine and visible way of life.

As James Jones writes in **Living the Gospel as a Way of Life**:

"Evangelization without the concrete witness of Christian love is why many attempts at renewal have an abstract, theoretical ring to them – lots of programs, little context; lots of doing but precious little being. In the end, we have nothing to sell, not even Jesus; all we can offer is an invitation to a relationship with the God who has decided to pitch His tent among sinners. . . Insofar as we are striving to grow in the fruit of the Holy Spirit . . . and in the hope of our confession, people will be drawn to Christ and His Gospel. Despite our manifold and only-too-apparent inadequacies, they'll come and they'll see."

This means, in many cases, that it is more imperative than ever that we take the need to restore Christian culture seriously. We must recreate elements of the support systems and family culture that undergirded practical Christian life in the past, in order to make our relationships real, that is, a practical reality lived out in the world, rather than an abstract or largely private ideal. Needless to say, such a project involves much improvisation, much trial and error. And, it's worth noting, the willingness to make many, many mistakes.

One of the most surprising things we discovered in the course of these decades-long efforts to build community – full as they were (and are) of starts and stops, trial and error – was the central role the Lord's Day played in this whole spiritual/cultural enterprise.

The word "surprise" is apt. In the beginning, when we first started experimenting with various ways to set the Lord's Day apart, we had no idea that it would produce something other than perhaps a more "spiritual" way to spend weekends. What we found, instead, was:

- That establishing the custom of the Lord's Day was often the place to start for groups that wished to develop closer and more stable bonds, that the right things tended to happen, that the problem of "false intensity" and rigorism that tends to sink such attempts at the outset could be avoided by allowing the Lord's Day, with its culture of celebration, to be the formative influence.

- That the Lord's Day's regimen of prayer in the home influenced the character of the home itself, that it inspired developments in domestic piety on other days of the week, that it helped foster (and image) the evolution of an effective "domestic church."

- That the sometimes heroic efforts families made to "corral" older children into the mandatory Saturday-night-with-the-family ritual resulted, often enough, in perceptible changes within the family itself, in closer bonds of communication between parents and children, in the renewal of family meals on other nights of the week and in the restoration, in many cases, of a more active family life.

- That the act of turning off the TV and turning up the volume on life on the Lord's Day resulted, in some cases, in the revival of family activities, games, sports, and family-generated entertainment that made the family a <u>place of life</u>

once more, not merely a place to "crash" or a comfortable refuge from the vicissitudes of work.

- That the culture of celebration fostered on the Lord's Day evolved into a more generally celebrative culture within the community – into a deeper and more pervasive atmosphere of honor, appreciation, gratitude and love.

On this last point, I cannot resist telling a story from those early days about celebration that made a big impression on me. After the Lord's Day had been established as part of community life, I happened upon a couple of community friends who were on their way to dinner.

"What's the occasion?" I asked.

"Oh, Bob's just made a hard decision – a good one -- something that's going to mean a lot to his family one day. I just thought that called for a celebration. It's not every day a man gets up the courage to do the right thing!"

This is what Caryll Houselander meant in an earlier chapter when she writes about the "sacramentality" of everyday life – in this case, the idea that the proper response to someone's hard-won resolution or costly decision to repent might not be a brusque "pat on the back" but a celebration. See Luke 15 and the story of the Prodigal Son for details.

What we discovered over the decades was that the efforts required to make the Lord's Day an effective part of Christian life were the same efforts required to build community, to create vital Christian relationships. The Lord's Day, in this sense, proved to be both the seed of community life, and the icon or image of what the end result should look like – not only a good life in the here and now but a taste of <u>home</u>, of the heavenly Jerusalem to come.

"And I saw the holy city, New Jerusalem, coming down out of heaven from God, prepared as a bride adorned for her husband; and I heard a loud voice from the throne saying, 'Behold, the dwelling of God is with men. He will dwell with them and they shall be his people, and God himself will be with them; he will wipe away every tear from their eyes, and death shall be no more, neither shall there be mourning and crying nor pain any more, for the former things [the old order] has passed away.'" Revelation 21:1-4

Building Christian relationships is never easy, and, furthermore, never fully accomplished. We will fall into bad habits and fail in love to the end of our days. But what the Lord's Day culture of honor, gratitude, and celebration does is place <u>joy</u> at the heart of the process.

Bibliography

The Documents of Vatican II (Walter M. Abbott, editor), Herder & Herder, NY, 1966 (see *Liturgy,* chap. V:102-106).

Commentary on the Documents of Vatican II (Herbert Vorgrimler, editor), Herder & Herder, NY, 1966.

Agee, James, *A Death in the Family* (*Knoxville: Summer 1915*), Library of America, 2005. (pp. 469-473)

Bacchiocchi, Samuele, *From Sabbath to Sunday: A Historical Investigation of the Rise of Sunday Observance in Early Christianity*, Gregorian University Press, 1977.

Bouyer, Louis, *Liturgical Piety*, University of Notre Dame Press, (1955) 1978. (see chapter 14: "The Mystery of the Liturgical Year: The Easter Liturgy" and chapter 19: "The Mystery and the World")

The Catechism of the Catholic Church [CCC], Liguori Publications, 1994. (see pp. 523-529)

Danielou, Jean, *The Bible and the Liturgy*, University of Notre Dame Press, 2002. (see chapter 15: "The Lord's Day" and chapter 16: "The Eighth Day")

Eskenazi, Tamara C, Harrington, Daniel J, & Shea, William H. (editors): *The Sabbath in Jewish and Christian Tradition*, Crossroad, NY, 1991.

Heschel, Abraham Joshua, *The Sabbath: Its Meaning for Modern Man*, Farrar, Straus, and Giroux, NY, 1995.

Jungmann, Josef A., *The Early Liturgy to the Time of Gregory the Great*, University of Notre Dame Press, 1980. [reprint] (see chapter 3: "Sunday and Easter in the Primitive Church")

Pieper, Josef, *Leisure: The Basis of Culture*, Ignatius Press, 2009.

Inaugurating the Lord's Day

Gabriel Meyer described in general terms the custom of inaugurating the Lord's Day on Saturday evening with a special meal, including blessings, singing and honoring those sitting around the table. This tradition has become an important and beloved practice in the City of the Lord Covenant Community. We have created a website that provides many resources for those who might want to try out the Lord's Day dinner in their own homes. You get there through the City of the Lord website: **www.cityofthelord.org**, or by going to: **www.keepingholythelordsday.com**.

Living the Gospel as a Way of Life

If you enjoyed this book, you will want to read another book written by Jim Jones, one of the founders of City of the Lord, Phoenix, with Gabriel Meyer - **Living the Gospel as a Way of Life**, published in 2014. It is a reflection on the personal call to live as a disciple of Jesus Christ in the power of the Holy Spirit. The authors share much of the accumulated wisdom that comes from forty years of living a life together in covenant community. The book, along with a ten-part DVD series presented by co-author Gabriel Meyer, can be found through the City of the Lord website or by going to: **www.livingthegospelasawayoflife.com**.

www.ingramcontent.com/pod-product-compliance
Lightning Source LLC
Chambersburg PA
CBHW071329040426
42444CB00009B/2119